Diary of a Heretic!

The Pagan Adventures of a Christian Priest

Diary of a Heretic!

The Pagan Adventures of a
Christian Priest

Mark Townsend

MOON
BOOKS

Winchester, UK
Washington, USA

First published by Moon Books, 2013
Moon Books is an imprint of John Hunt Publishing Ltd., Laurel House, Station Approach,
Alresford, Hants, SO24 9JH, UK
office1@jhpbooks.net
www.johnhuntpublishing.com
www.moon-books.net

For distributor details and how to order please visit the 'Ordering' section on our website.

Text copyright: Mark Townsend 2013

ISBN: 978 1 78279 271 0

A CIP catalogue record for this book is available from the British Library.

Design: Stuart Davies

Printed and bound by CPI Group (UK) Ltd, Croydon, CR0 4YY

We operate a distinctive and ethical publishing philosophy in all
areas of our business, from our global network of authors to
production and worldwide distribution.

CONTENTS

Mark, your best stance is probably to be amused by it all, and then do whatever your guides guide you towards. Just avoid being defensive – they are used to being Persecutors who set up defensive Victims, so hold yourself above all that. Stay centered in love, and humour, and openness and honesty. And enjoy your new status as a heretic priest!

Gill Edwards (RIP), author of *Living Magically, Stepping into the Magic, Pure Bliss, Wild Love, Life Is A Gift* and *Conscious Medicine*

To Sally, the woman I spent all my life waiting to meet.
Now that I have, I am grateful beyond words.
I love you from the bottom of my heart.
X

Acknowledgments

The first person I wish to thank is the Barefoot Doctor, Stephen Russell, for his incredible Foreword. I've had the pleasure of Stephen's company and he's one of those people who oozes natural wisdom, yet never makes you feel inferior. Within seconds of meeting him I knew I could be totally myself, nothing hidden.

Then, for her invaluable editing and constant supply of suggestions and advice (throughout the whole process), much appreciation goes to *Donata Ahern*, a wise woman and initiate of many sacred paths.

Huge gratitude also goes to Philip Carr-Gomm, who stopped me from making the mistake of sending off the MS before it was ready. He read it through and, after a long phone conversation, I knew what needed to be done.

Thanks also go to my many friends on Facebook and the online community we call Hedge-Church, for their willingness to watch and comment on the process as it took place. Often I would test out various extracts, and the online encouragement has been immense.

Thank you to all the people of the various spiritual and religious groups of which I belong: The Open Episcopal Church, The Progressive Christian Alliance, The Progressive Christianity Network Britain, The Order of Bards, Ovates and Druids, The Dudeist Organisation and Hedge-Church.

I want to acknowledge the denomination that first ordained me too, The Church of England. I've said many times that I will always love her, my original spiritual Mother. No matter how frustrated I was as one of her priests, and no matter how hurt I still am by our battered relationship, I remain deeply loyal to the core tradition of Anglicanism, which (at its best) is inclusive, tolerant, intelligent and all embracing.

I have dedicated this book to my beautiful Sally, but I also wish to thank her here for her unfailing support of my ministry and work. I genuinely could not have got through the last year without her. I lost the ability to drive any real distance and she became my unofficial and ever willing chauffeur. What an angel.

And finally to my children, Aisha and Jamie, two gemstones who never fail to impress me with their natural wisdom, creative imaginations and darn right loveliness.

Mark Townsend

Prologue

Roughly fifteen years ago I had a nervous breakdown. I was a Church of England vicar at the time and had to be signed off work and put on a course of antidepressants with counselling. The demands from both the church and myself (my own projected self-expectations) where just too great and I was falling apart. Also my marriage was failing big time. My kids are the gemstones of my life, but I'm afraid their mum and me were simply incompatible. So it all crumbled and I (recklessly) let my heart out to a member of the congregation, a woman! I guess you can imagine where this all ended? When we are messed about, hurting and frightened, we do crazy things.

About seven years after this, and well after the relationship had come to an end, I decided to "confess" it all to my bishop. As a result I had to resign.

Though self-indulgent, I find the reflecting upon and writing of my own story to be one of the most therapeutic and psychologically beneficial pursuits in life. I thoroughly recommend it to everyone. The process usually begins when I'm running in the morning, as if the rhythmic jogging loosens and churns up the clay in my mind and allows the contents to be processed bit by bit. It's like taking a metaphorical mesh bottomed garden sieve and plunging it deep into the soil of life, gently sieving through all the various elements, pondering, gazing, harmonizing, re-assessing and eliminating as it moves through the wire net and falls back out to fertilize and benefit the flower beds below.

It's a process of both pain and pleasure, of discomfort and discovery, for you end up with two different products (apart from all the newly sieved soil that falls back on the garden). You are left with both muck and magic, chunks of large, sharp and seemingly dangerous rock, and among them tiny nuggets of glittering gold and perhaps even the odd diamond or two.

I've left both the muck and the magic within the diary you are about to read. The reason is simple; you can often only find the diamonds when you've been honest about the crap. And you need to see this as an authentic and honest telling of my story; otherwise you will end up with nothing more than a half truth which is, in effect, an untruth.

Foreword

Seems to me everyone – and I include myself in this – are caught in a vain and constant striving for perfection. We strive to be perfect, as if redeeming ourselves in the eyes of our maker, omitting to acknowledge that our maker, whether you call the primordial generator of life Existence, God, Tao, or Whatever, has, so to speak, made us as we are: a composite of yin and yang, dark and light, messy and miraculous – because that's the way we're meant to be.

Accepting this relieves layers of undue stress instantly. And as far as I can see from my own personal process, and from having worked or been in touch with millions of people around the planet in various states of distress over the past few decades, releasing stress as we go along to prevent accumulation is paramount to attaining and sustaining health in the mind, in the body and in our relationship with existence.

In any case, would the maker, no matter what you called it, nor through which framework you addressed it, expect us to be perfect, other than in the perfectly imperfect, or imperfectly perfect way we already are?

Would the maker expect anything whatsoever? I don't think so. The maker isn't a person. I suggest the maker doesn't default to humanoid habits like expecting things. The maker merely is. The maker merely 'makes'. Presumably it's precisely for this reason it squeezes and contorts itself, via the long and arduous process of evolution, into forms like ours in the first place: so it *can* experience these very human sensations - *through* us.

It's us who project these human qualities, we who anthropo-morphise the maker, simply because, unless engaged in some sort of ongoing process of daily meditation (in the broadest sense), whereby we're able to regularly transcend the merely human level of cognition, we know no other way to make sense of the ineffable. Indeed I believe the biblical notion that God made man in His own image was meant in reverse: man-made God in *his* own image.

Nonetheless on we go wasting inordinate amounts of crucial vital force fighting with ourselves for not being perfect.

Despite our aspirations, so unremittingly compounded by a media and advertising industry that depends for its existence on persuading us to keep buying products or experiences that will *make* us perfect, the truth is, no matter what we buy, no matter whether shoes or facelifts, we're all flawed, we're all with our inner mechanisms broken in myriad ways: we're all works in progress.

If healing is to be achieved, if we're to grow into anywhere near the fullness of ourselves, the process must be instigated, not just once, but continually with a near as possible honest self-appraisal and acceptance of these flaws and glitches.

What Mark does here, with admirable courageousness, is lay himself fully bare and disclose his own flaws and glitches, not in a mawkish or confessional way, not seeking forgiveness or acceptance, but in order to inspire the reader to do likewise.

He invites and encourages us to make peace with the inevitable string of failures and messes that occur in every life, rather than mask them for shame, or to fit in to the general mesh of masking, obfuscation and lies that commonly passes for currency in society's intrinsic warp and weft.

In this world of pretence and artifice we need as much help finding our authenticity as we can get.

I've had the privilege of spending time with Mark and whether seen through the prism of Christianity, Druidism or just basic humanitarianism, he's certainly a fitting exemplar of the priest archetype, but more importantly is a genuine man of God.

It shines from him as a visible light.

He's clearly here to serve us all in helping us grow into the unmitigated fullness of ourselves in all our fractured power and glory and so facilitate a more harmonious world for everyone.

I'm honoured to be the one he's chosen to blow the trumpet and invite you to share the same privilege of spending some time with him in this wonderful book.

Stephen Russell - The Barefoot Doctor

Introduction

Reality shall set you free.

I've never forgotten those words. I think it was the hilarious writer Adrian Plass who re-interpreted the famous words of Jesus in such a way, or was he quoting someone else? It doesn't matter. The fact is that "reality" is a much more vivid word to help understand the phrase than "truth." Truth can so often come across as a forensic and intolerant word, conjuring up images of those sour faced bin bag Christian protesters who stand on the roadside shaking their fists as Gay Pride enthusiasts march past. Their black plastic dustbin liner clothing is often painted with large white words forming vile sentences about truth, heresy and hell fire.

Reality is indeed a much better word than truth. Reality *shall* set you free. Reality is about what *really is, what really is true*. Truth can so often be something you try with all your might to believe, but deep down you know is a pile of crap. It hurts; it seriously hurts the soul to cling to stuff that is not really you. And it's dishonest; it's living a lie. Many religious people try so damned hard to believe the truth because they think it will set them free, but instead they erect dirty great prison walls around themselves. The fact is that such "truth" does not set you free, and when you come to see this, then (ironically) you *have* been set free.

So is this book about freedom? Well yes in a way it is, though that's just the beginning. It's about a life set free and how such freedom (won in a most unpleasant manner) can lead to the most awesome adventures, as long as you stay within the fragile yet blessed place of authenticity (reality). This is a book that follows what is a messy and, at the same time, magical journey of a priest who was asked to resign from ministry after he made a confession to do with something which haunted him (the full story is told in my book *The Path of the Blue Raven* chapter six).

I decided not to be too worried about the nit picking conventions of pen-craft and simply let each moment speak for itself, so I have literally followed my own progress over the course of a year. There are high points and there are low points. There are "ah ha" moments of pure magic, and there are transformative discoveries. There is also much expressed inner debate and confusion. I wanted this book to offer similarly broken, confused and fallen people a little light, a little hope. I want to encourage all those beaten up by their projected self-expectations to stick in there and believe that *all* things can work together for good. I want this book to bring a sense of hope and grace to all those who, like me, have made mistakes, suffered falls and made bad choices that fill the heart with regret and shame. Believe me, I've made some serious mistakes in the past, and I have suffered the consequences of being honest about them to those who were in control of my life. Yet the simple fact that I was honest about them unlocked the prison doors of my psyche and set me free.

I want the following pages to encourage and inspire self-honesty within *your* life situation for I have discovered how liberating an authentic and open life can be.

Painful? Yes.

At times disorientating? Yes.

Frightening? Yes.

Sacrificial? Most definitely.

Yet also liberating beyond measure.

Finally, for the words ahead to make sense you'll need to be aware of a few points:

Alongside my battered Christian priesthood I am a Stage Magician (illusionist) and a member of a Druid Order (a nature based spiritual tradition). My goal has been to discover a way forward that honours each of these three strands and sees them as complimentary rather than oppositional.

Also the year that I recorded for this book was 2009, which I chose because it immediately followed one of the most depressing and traumatic years of my entire life. I "went to hell and back" in 2008, due to the impact of my resignation and consequent pressures that stemmed from that decision. So I started a diary in January 2009 to try to process and make sense of what was happening to me. As it turned out 2009 was also pretty horrible. At times I felt totally crushed by the weight of it.

However, it's now five years later and many things have changed in my life situation. So, during the editing process I felt I had to remove various elements. I simply couldn't leave in every aspect of the story because there are people to protect. I've removed many of the references to other individuals and have left my own closest ones almost completely out of it.

On top of this, because of my deep belief in the need to be honest about my faults, much of what I've left in may come across as unnecessarily childish. I realise there is a risk of being misunderstood, but I want my readers to *feel* the utter despair (even though you have to sometimes remain only partially aware of what, or who, *caused* that despair). As I've already said, I want to show how diamonds can sparkle and glitter the most brightly when they lie within the rubble of life. It's the only way. There's no point pretending, and there's far too much pretence in the spiritual/religious world. Sugary books claiming that life is perfect and you can constantly live on a bed of roses are no help to anyone, *period!*

Finally, I make many references to my other books and use some ideas, phrases and terms from them. While it's not necessary to have read any of those books to understand this one, it is probably helpful to know the following:

The Gospel of Falling Down

Part of the thesis of the above book is that each of us have two inner voices; what Jungian psychologists refer to as the ego and the self, and what some spiritual teachers refer to as the False-Self and the True or God-Self. Within the book I refer to them as the Little-Me (ego) and the Divine-Me (self), and I see the Little-Me as the voice (or "collection of voices") which tend to rule our thoughts and are basically self-protecting, attention seeking, praise demanding and defensive. Whereas the Divine-Me is the deeper, wiser and usually unnoticed voice of wisdom that exists underneath all the mental clutter of the ego's noise. In the book I gave a few exercises that enable people to get in touch with these different aspects of our characters and, when people do, it can be a massive revelation. I also talk about the natural dialogues I've found myself involved in, usually through my writing, when the two voices seem to correspond. I included some of these dialogues within *The Gospel of Falling Down* as examples. Since the point when I first recognised these voices I've become more and more aware of what I call the Divine-Me. When the Divine-Me is expressed within this book it will be through an *italic* font.

The Wizard's Gift

The Wizard's Gift book is a parable of the inner voices I just mentioned. It is a novel about a suicidal man who meets a wise old wizard within the very forest where he attempts to end his life. The consequent story is his gradual getting to know the wizard and learning from his wisdom. It concludes with some thoughts about the "Inner Wizard" or the "Wizard Within" as a reality that we all possess. It is the same voice as the Divine-Me.

Another important point, which is implicit within both the above books, is that the magical gift of this wise inner voice is often revealed within the mess, muddle and brokenness of life.

The Path of the Blue Raven

Rather than giving a summary of the above book it will make much more sense to quote something from it:

I've always believed that one of the church's primary functions is to do with embracing the fallen and dispensing grace. However the truth is that while priest Mark Townsend never had a problem with offering grace to other messy souls he just couldn't seem to do the same for himself. In the end the mess and unhappiness from his own journey proved too burdensome to be able to continue as a priest.

Consequences follow actions. It's one of life's most basic laws. We reap what we sow. This is one major reason why I refuse to hold on to the petty grudges and feelings of hostility towards those who've hurt me. Revenge is like drinking rat poison in an effort to kill the damn rodent. Venom, let loose, will only end up poisoning us.

But I didn't need rat poison to hurt me. I had a habit of turning my anger and pain inward. So back in 2007 I decided to do something very risky, to put my money where my mouth was and unburden myself not to another anonymous counsellor, family member or friend, but to someone within the ecclesiastical world whose opinion I would have no option but to take note of. I needed to be brave enough to share all my shit and mess with this person and not only that, do whatever he recommended. That was my condition to myself.

I was about to move to a new post within the church but my heart told me I needed to do something before I could feel free to be Installed. It all has to do with that word authenticity again. In order to be made the new Priest in Charge, I would have to go through a ceremony where, among other things, I would be required to submit to the authority of both the bishop and the Queen (church and state). The bishop would end the ceremony by giving me his blessing for my future as someone who shared his "cure of souls." Both my previous Installation ceremonies were under my previous bishop's reign.

Well, my heart simply would not let me go through all this

until I'd looked my bishop in the eye and allowed him to see the "real Mark." I knew that I would need to make something of a confession to him, and tell him about all the mess and muddle of the previous few years. There was literally no other way. I do believe in transparency, especially within the context of such situations as this. The problem was that one particular part of this mess was "big stuff." Sure, I'd talked it through (and even made confessions) many times before (even to the church hierarchy) but this man was my new Father in God. I simply could not stand before him, feel his hand of blessing on my head, and know that my sorry story was a secret.

I sought councel from half a dozen or so trusted friends in dog collars. Only one of them thought I should do it. The rest said that, while my "mess" was something that probably a quarter of the clergy of the land had (at some point) made, there was no point bringing up the past when it could threaten my future. I disagreed. A future would be no future at all if it were not authentic. I needed to risk everything in order to gain freedom. The freedom might have also included a new post in the country or it might not.

Thus I found myself sat in front of my bishop making what was essentially a confession about my past. I cannot tell the whole tale here for it is not mine alone to tell. However I can say that some of it was to do with a relationship I'd gotten into with a married woman. By that time it had been over for almost a couple of years but it still haunted me.

To this day I am deeply ashamed of what I did, and am truly sorry for the obvious pain I caused. But we humans are a mixture of light and dark. And when life gets hard, and dreams are shattered, we can react in foolish and selfish ways. I was messed up and allowed myself to get attached to a sympathetic soul, but it was wrong and I take full responsibility for my actions, *which is why I never ended up moving to that new post.*

The long and the short of it is that I was asked to resign for a period of three years. I can't pretend it wasn't a bombshell.

I'm not writing any of this because I have any blame towards anyone (apart from myself). The reason for allowing this part of the story to have a place is so that the rest of the book rings true and is authentic. *My* mistake all those years ago, and *my* decision to let my boss know about it, changed the very shape of my future.

Extract taken from Path of the Blue Raven: From Religion to Re-enchantment, (published Nov. 2009 buy O-Books).

January

It's a new year, thank God! Now I can at last slam the door on the last one. Bang! I need to hold it tight, lean against it and stop any of the poison creeping through. I imagine it trying to find a crack, like some noxious green Gotham City gas that's found its way to the air vent. If a year could be personified then 2008 is Jack Nicolson's Joker dressed as an old fashioned puppet master, complete with a marionette figurine on strings. And who is this effigy? Me of course. And up above my head dances the laughing green-haired-psycho slamming me into one calamity after another.

I can visualise the other guy coming out of the dark, the man who thinks he is a bat. There he is and he's holding a sharp bat handled blade. Swish! Bye bye Joker!

The door's closed. The strings have been cut. Last year is gone, and here I am ready for a fresh new year and a chance to win a little happiness.

Okay, so I just exaggerated a little. Last year was dreadful but it was not all bad. I learned many invaluable lessons too. And a new year brings with it a fresh sense of hope. I just wonder what this year will bring for me and my family. It feels a whole lot different to this time last year. How on earth we got through it I'll never know, *but we did.*

* * *

Nothing's permanent. Everything is constantly changing, developing, mutating and being transformed. And all this change and necessary growth is painful. It requires many deaths. There is no other way. Life, death and re-birth is nature's on-going cycle of creation, destruction and re-creation. We can't halt the process just because we don't like it. In fact, when we get in the way of nature, she fights back.

Today the last branch of dear old *Woolies* closed. For a hundred years we've had Woolworths in our towns and cities. It's almost as established as the dear old Church of England. What's happening? More and more businesses are throwing in their hands every day. It's an economic melt-down. Is that all part of nature fighting back? Is there some deeper reason why we are waving goodbye to so much of what we've known? Are we so overgrown in our bulging, pulsating cities that the only possible way forward is a severe pruning back of dead wood? Have we attempted to re-build Babel as a strange post-religious temple to the gods of secular capitalism? And has the tower begun to crumble under its own colossal weight?

* * *

It's only the first week in the New Year and already I'm faced with a probable controversy. I wrote a strong but genuinely well intentioned letter to the local press just before Christmas. I was upset by the remarks made by the Pope that were interpreted as him drawing a parallel between homosexuality and the destruction of the rain forests. Today's newspaper has dropped through the post and there it is, the top headline, staring at me from the floor. *They turned my letter into a front page article:*

Ex-Vicar Slams Pope's Anti-Gay Message

The article continues:

A North Herefordshire clergyman, who uses magic tricks to spread his religious message, has spoken out in defense of gay priests as a row caused by the Pope's comments on homosexuality rumbles on.

As gay groups and activists reacted angrily to Pope Benedict XVI's claims that saving humanity from homosexual or trans-sexual behaviour must rank on the same scale as protecting the environment, Rev Mark Townsend expressed dismay at the end of year speech to staff at the Vatican.

No stranger to controversy himself, Mr. Townsend, who gave up his job with the Herefordshire Diocese to carry out spiritual work with the aid of magic, explained that some of his best friends are gay Catholic and Anglican priests. "I thank God for the ministry of every one of them, and I make this point because, should either the Roman or Anglican church ever succeed in eliminating all gay men and women from the ranks of the clergy – well, I'm afraid large areas of the church would cease to exist, for there would be no-one left to serve them," he stated.

The former team ministry leader, who was vicar at Leominster Priory Church for eight years, makes it clear the views are his own, and not those of the Church of England or Hereford Diocese.

"I do not speak for them. I speak as a flawed and imperfect ex-vicar, with pagan leanings, who still loves the church but hates its exclusivity," he said.

He believed Pope Benedict did not intend his remarks to be 're-expressed' the way they were. "But even if you water it down, to see homosexuality as such a threat to the institution of the church boggles the mind," he said. "What a 'wonderful' message from the world's most prominent church leader!"

The UK Lesbian and Gay Christian Movement called the Pope's remarks "irresponsible and unacceptable."

Mr. Townsend said: "I have been a priest for 10 years, and over the course of that period, have had the privilege of getting to know some truly wonderful clergy, Roman, Anglican and Protestant, and an enormous percentage of them are gay. I have been taught by them, trained alongside them, worked with them, been absolved by them, laughed with them and cried with them."

"Surely our founder, the one whose birthday we have just celebrated, taught that love, rather than judgement is the way?"

I bet that goes down like a lead balloon! It reminds me of last year when a very tongue in cheek letter of mine ended up with my receiving a hierarchical phone call and a demand for a letter of apology to an offended Christian couple who'd written a complaint about me. Okay it was a silly letter, but understandable bearing in mind the circumstances. I'd been attacked in the local newspaper three times over one of my books. A fundamentalist Christian had complained that my book was dangerous heresy. I politely replied, showing respect for his opinion. He wrote another attack. Again I replied politely, and he responded with yet another attack. So I wrote this: "If Jesus ever decided to come back to earth he'd probably take one look and say 'Screw the church' and go down the pub for a real conversation."

The next thing I heard was an episcopal voice on the phone saying that he'd received a complaint about me and that I must apologise by letter. He also said, "Mark the church is the bride of Christ." I felt like saying, "Well in that case maybe Jesus wants a divorce," but I bit my tongue instead.

* * *

Peter Owen Jones's new BBC television series has begun. It's brave and breath-taking! This eccentric vicar's TV appearances are one of the very few public portrayals of the Church of England that give me any hope for the future of British Anglicanism. But I wonder how long he'll get away with pushing the boundaries the way he does. I've been looking forward to this ever since I first heard about it. I thought his previous series *Extreme Pilgrim* was one of the best pieces of religious broadcasting ever. It was open, gutsy, exciting, spiritual, dynamic, realistic and thoroughly human.

What's astonishing about the first episode of *Around the World in 80 Faiths* is the undeniable fact that so much natural Paganism still makes meaning all over the world, even within strictly monotheistic cultures. There were examples of both Christian and Islamic communities that have clearly continued some of their pre-monotheistic Pagan practises, and even found ways to incorporate them into their current religious culture and practices.

* * *

I have three funerals on at the moment and was particularly moved by a visit I made to a family yesterday. The widow told of how her late husband's only concern was with regard to who would officiate at his funeral. He and his wife had ceased to be religious after their children had grown up, but they always remained open to spiritual things. He knew that the "done thing" was to have the local vicar officiate. The other option would have been a humanist, but that would rule out any prayers or hymns.

The widow said, "Then Victoria found you, Mark, our answer." [Victoria is the funeral director] I can't express how humbling and awe inspiring it is to still be used in this way. I hope I never stop thinking of this as the most awesome privilege.

An ingredient that contributes much to my ceremonies is the Druidry I've been immersed within. The Order of Bards, Ovates and Druids has given me so much over the last couple of years. Pagan Druidry adds what is lacking within regular Christian worship and practise; a deep love and reverence for nature, a recognition and appreciation of the divine feminine, an earthy and dramatic use of metaphor, symbol and ritual, and much more.

I've begun a new pattern of prayer too but don't be misled by the use of the term "new." It's not as if there was an *old* pattern. My regular prayer routine began to fade shortly after my resignation in June 2007. Throughout last year I took regular trips to the forest to sit, contemplate, whine, and occasionally listen to the "voice within," but as for formal "prayer times," not interested. Church rarely saw me either. However I do feel the time has come to plug myself back in to some daily rhythm; not a proscribed dogmatism, but a gentle setting aside of a few choice moments as a spiritual heart beat for the week. I'm using my friend Rev. Tess Ward's beautiful book *The Celtic Wheel of the Year*. This book is a treasure chest, drawing upon both Christian and Pagan sources. So far so good, I've kept it up really well, *but then it is only the 7th Jan*.

* * *

I just dropped my gorgeous kids at the school bus stop. How lucky I am to have them. They teach me so much, and are so different to how I was as a boy. A right little "so and so" I was:

[*Ding dong!*] '*agggggggggh, what have you done now Mark?*'

That was the sound of my mum who, about thirty-seven years ago opened the door on her eight year old son. He'd been playing with his chemistry set again. Why the hell did they give those things to kids back then? There I was, chimp's grin across my face, hands burning like a flaming torch from *Raiders of the Lost Ark*. I'd soaked my hand in methylated spirit and set it alight with a match. I realised that if you kept your hand flapping, the wind would cool your hand as the spirit burnt off (before scorching the skin). I did get hurt a few times with my silly games but it was fun.

What a contrast to the control freak I turned into.

* * *

I'm walking down *The Grange*, a lovely park area near the church I used to be vicar of. I love my morning walks. Not long ago I spotted a raven couple down near the river. Funnily enough I was by some standing stones when I saw them. Since then the two beautiful black angels have occasionally appeared, croaking and flying acrobatically across the sky. I hope I see them today. There are always plenty of crows but these magic black ravens are rare and awesome. It was a raven vision that inspired my last book.

The rest of the feathered tribe is loud today, audibly decorating the otherwise silent dawn with an array of happy voices. I love the way nature speaks. More and more I find the Druidic way of appreciating the divinity of the natural world so appealing.

I blessed my home yesterday, with a Druid ritual. I've done home blessings before but they seem to come from the perspective of places being somehow "dark" until you claim it for the light, as if the house is both being blessed and exorcised at the same time. I find other sacraments similar, like baptism. In fact many do see baptism as a mini service of deliverance. The baby is somehow cleansed and brought into the light. I've never viewed it in this way. To me a baptism is a marking out of whatever already is true. My Druid home blessing was, likewise, a celebration of the gift of the space (which is already good) and a blessing of the Great Spirit upon it. Naturally there are also notions of protection within the rite but not with the heavy dark and light dualism.

* * *

I'm beginning to feel a little more settled in my unsettledness. Faith, let's face it, is a slippery business. Trying to hold on to it with certainty is like trying to hold onto a bar of soap in a bath. Faith is riddled with doubt, confusion, at times despair, and has the inevitable smattering of hypocrisy.

The church is still (at least partially) my spiritual family (though they, Christians, scare the crap out of me at times). I'm even preparing to perform as a magician at a couple of Diocesan Conventions this year; the first is only a few days away [shudder!]. It's for the Diocese of Rochester. I've been invited to perform a magic show as their final entertainment. It should be fun, but before that I'm off to do the same thing at a church in Birmingham, at the parish of St. Francis of Assisi, Bourneville. My friends from Theological College are in ministry there. Peter is the vicar and his wife Paula is the Reader (as well as being one of the most well respected theologians in the Church of England). She taught me Old Testament at theological college and was fantastic. We hung off every word. Her lectures were passionate and engaging.

* * *

I'm down *The Grange* again. The orchestra is in full swing this morning. Birds of every variety make music to the dawn and humanity's mechanical music compliments: the distant grinding of lorries on the busy bypass and a car pulling into a driveway close by. The coarse, yet wondrous crow's caw, the soft coo coo of the wood pigeon above my head, cushioned beneath a blanket of sound from the smaller tweeting birds; the tits and finches. Birds have a powerful divinatory significance within modern Druidry. My own soul-bird, the raven, is seen as a magical creature, symbolic of spiritual transformation. For centuries these carrion eating birds have been associated with the corpses of the battle field and thus have an interpretation similar to that of the tarot death card – *the dying of a past aspect of your life and re-birth into a completely new life.*

Now the great Priory's bell gongs eight times. It reminds me of the eight years I was its vicar. This is the very building where I'd lean over the altar rail to distribute communion and (more importantly to me) kneel down to bless those who'd *not* been confirmed. I miss it. A lump comes to my throat as I think of the great privilege of being a priest for people, real people. Part of the job today means being a priest of an increasingly irrelevant institution, but there's still much importance involved in parish ministry; holding families and individuals through tough and tearful times, being there to bless and welcome new life into this world, and helping make some sense of life for those who have all but given up!

I swallow, dislodge the lump, and whisper a prayer of thanks to the Great Mystery who's moved me on to deeper things, magical truths and more privileges of serving this fragile world. No longer do I have to suffer the futile games of the institution.

* * *

I went out on the town for a few beers tonight and bumped into a young crowd who were watching a lad do some sleight of hand magic. He was good. They saw me and asked me to show them something but I pointed at the guy and said *"he's* your magician." But then even he demanded that I perform. So I did a few effects. I have a rule here: always encourage, never put down and never show off. Share the magic and leave it with the audience. Don't snatch it back when you finish as if it's your possession. Magic was there before you arrived and remains there after you've gone. Your role is simply to uncover it for them.

* * *

I was thinking about revenge today, mainly because I'd had a chat with a very angry and aggressive woman; someone who takes no prisoners. One rule I hope I always manage to stick to is this: never deal out "like for like." Though the temptation will at times be intense, it will only be returned with even greater force. Hatred only breeds more hatred. Bless don't curse. Curses contain a sinister sticky substance that stains the curser as much as the one being cursed. Be honest. Yes, say if something has hurt you, but do not retaliate with vengefulness. Let love be the inner guide. Fear is the poison of the soul. It manifests in violence, either literal violence or violent thoughts, and both can kill.

* * *

I'm back down *The Grange* again and I just noticed a mass of sprouting shoots. Mother Earth is already preparing her spring time flower festival. Who can claim poverty when we have such riches under our feet? I don't think I need much more than this right now.

* * *

I'm preparing a funeral for a man of nature, a man who spent his whole life in ecology and conservation with a particular interest in birds. He did not follow a religious path. His dear wife wants to reflect his passion for nature within the ceremony and needs it to be honest and authentic. It will be a ceremony at the local woodland burial site. This is what I have decided to say as part of the introductory words:

> *This ceremony, though nonreligious, will be deeply spiritual, and Peter's warm and generous character will shine through it all. Whatever we think or feel about the spiritual world it surely cannot only be locked away inside a book or a building. So today we meet outside, under the canopy of the sky; within the natural temple of the woodland, among the fellow devotees of the birds, rabbits, deer and all the other creatures of the forest.*

* * *

I'm sitting in a beautiful holy place, the church of St. Francis of Assisi, Bourneville, Birmingham. I just nipped into the side chapel and found myself genuflecting in front of the tabernacle. Looks like the Catholic spirit is still alive inside me!

I've always had a soft spot for St. Francis. It's not just his creation-centred tradition that makes me buzz; it's the fact that he was so counter-cultural, even counter to the *church's* culture. He said "bugger progress, bugger selfish ambition, bugger success, bugger hierarchy, palaces, career clergy, huge cathedrals and so on." Well maybe he didn't quite put it that way but he *was* sure that such things were of no real importance. He knew that true freedom and thus true soulfulness was not about climbing ladders of achievement but by falling from those ladders and abandoning oneself to providence.

Peter, the vicar here, is a great guy. I do admire the grass roots parish clergy. I still think there are many heroes among them. They have more and more demands yet continue to give sacrificially.

Prayers have just begun in the side chapel and I've heard my name being mentioned. I'm here to perform my full evening show. My heart still beats in time to the Anglican heartbeat. I still breathe in the Anglican spirit. I just can't seem to find God in the creeping exclusivity that is taking over so much of the Church of England.

* * *

I feel so inspired by my Druidic encounters. I no longer subscribe to or feel moved by an Almighty God *up there*, only knowable through the blood of his son. I am no longer convinced by the story, the all-powerful and all-male monotheistic God who sits alone, separated from His creation, with the flawed followers below all struggling and striving to gain his approval. This is an image of a God who sends his son to bridge the gap *in blood!*

I just don't buy it anymore. I've not rejected the *whole* Christian story for there's much beauty within it, but the classic fall/redemption model is defunct in my opinion. However, to me Jesus is still a powerful symbol of the good-ness and god-ness of all people. He was a bringer of light and his gift was to give people back to themselves, rather than set up a human/divine exchange system. He *loved* people into the kingdom by demonstrating the deep love of the divine, which is unconditional and ever flowing. The angry God who demands a price (a blood bargain) for our sins just does not make sense.

To me, Spirit (he, she, it) exists in and through and with and around all people and all creation. Over the millennia various cultures have tapped into this divine current and sought to express it in a multitude of ways, usually reflecting the landscape and culture of its origin. Faith grows out of the land that births it and nurtures it. If not a pantheist I am most certainly now a pan*en*theist for I see deity in all things.

So, can I still also hold onto my Christian identity? I believe I can, for the beauty of the Druidic approach is to see all systems as valid. Reading the mythologist Joseph Campbell has helped me greatly in this respect. He helps us to see that religious faith is not only quite natural but is also basically mythological. Myth does not mean falsehood; in fact it means the reverse, truth. Myth is truth told in story form. Myth expresses truth by metaphor, ritual and symbol. The Christian myth is what keeps me from abandoning the world of Christianity altogether.

* * *

I love bringing magic into people's lives. I do not see myself as a magician who *makes* magic, so much as a magician who awakens people to the magic they already possess. I waken the sleeping Merlin who lives inside us all.

Yet my magic is changing. I've noticed how (illusion) magic has the capacity to awaken people to inner (real) magic. I've noticed how the opening up of the intuitive and enchanted mindset encourages the occurrence of synchronicities. I've witnessed it happening more and more. Sometimes when I'm performing, I can stop doing the tricks, sit back and watch the magic take place without any help from me. Maybe this is why divinatory tools like the I Ching and the Tarot work for so many people. I've been fascinated by tarot for years. This year I hope to learn much more about their magic. Someday I want to write a hero-myth based on the characters of the major arcana.

I hope my spiritual wanderings don't mean my close friends in the church disown me. I still have many within ministry. I am their brother. I hope they will always see me the same way, no matter how far I stray. It's been tough explaining it to some of them.

* * *

Peter Owen Jones's second programme has just been on, *Wow*. The man is doing so much good. At last the general public can watch a Church of England vicar truly opening up to the wonder outside not just Anglican but *Christian* doors. He's a brave guy.

I'm now sitting in another church where I'm about to perform. I can hear the parrot fashion chanting of the Apostles Creed. Creeds were, I guess, part of the necessary containment imposed upon early Christianity. But I can't help seeing them as one more nail in the church's coffin of irrelevance. Creeds kill creativity. The minute we impose such limits on God/dess we've de-deified him/her for sure. How can a God be limited by the mere human beings who invented their religion in the first place?

* * *

I've been invited to be godfather to my two new twin nieces. What an honour. Of course I will say yes. I once conducted an outdoor baby naming ceremony while I was still a curate. It was magical and non-religious, yet they appointed godparents to the children. It's still a very good institution, the godparent. It's a beautiful thing when respected.

* * *

I'm back at *The Grange*. It's very early and I can see a near full moon. It's to my left as I sit. No wonder the ancients saw her as a goddess.

Today I'm visiting two extraordinary women who work within the world of global spirituality and mythology. The way I came across them was highly synchronistic. I'd been looking at my publisher's website forum and noticed an American site called spiritualwriters.com. It was asking for submissions, so I decided to send off some information on my books. The site's owner liked my work and the ethos behind it. She then suggested that I made contact with one of her friends (somewhere) here in the UK. She said I'd be very excited by her work. I looked up her website and found it fascinating. It was all about world mythology, the subject I'd been immersed within. I thought to myself *I have to visit her and see the exhibition,* but I had no idea where in the UK she was based. I imagined it would be London or some other important and progressive city hundreds of miles away.

I did some internet searching and finally came across details of the postal address for this amazing work. It turned out to be Kinnersley Castle, about seven miles from where I live.

* * *

I'm sitting in my car at a cemetery, preparing for a funeral at the woodland burial site. I can see the family and know I'm going to cry when this is over. Funerals are always emotional, but when you see a little boy who's lost his dad it breaks your heart.

I was once told not to get emotionally involved at funerals or during the preparation of them. What a stupid rule to teach. It goes without saying that you ought to be able to keep some sort of control, but how can you *not* get emotionally involved? We serve *by* making ourselves vulnerable. We hold and heal and make sense by feeling and empathising (at least in some small way) with the families *where they are*. I've sat with a dying boy, his family all around, tears streaming down my face. The little lad was holding tightly to the wooden cross I'd given him on a previous visit. It was a heart-breaking situation and his family did not want some detached and forensic man of religion. They wanted a pastor who cared, who felt, who loved, who knew what pain is like and was not afraid to show it.

A man I have always admired (in fact a priest who gave up his own ministry because he could not face taking any more money from an institution that treats gay people the way it does) once began a deeply traumatic funeral service with the following words, "Isn't God a shit." Of course he was not actually holding God responsible for the death, but was expressing what the family themselves had expressed to him. It's what being a priest is about.

* * *

I feel so honoured. I've just been invited to dedicate the new Priory church window in honour of Ron Barrington the dear ex-church warden who, with his wonderful wife Ann, was always so supportive of me when I was Team vicar of that church. He died from a serious heart condition. Sadly it's the same day as my two new nieces' baptisms, the ones I'm going to be Goddad to, but I am so touched that I was invited. I miss Ron.

* * *

President Barack Obama has just given his presidential inauguration address and rarely have I been so captivated and astonished by a speech. My prayer for him and his family has been replicated by folk all over the world in different ways: "May God protect them!"

* * *

I've just been asked to handfast a couple on an ITV programme. They are still married to their previous partners so it could be problematic but, if it goes ahead, the ceremony will be amazing. It's going to be held in the forest with Morris men, medieval music and the bride arriving on a white unicorn. *I hope it happens*.

* * *

What an extraordinary experience! I'm at the Butlins holiday resort at Bognor Regis and have just performed for the Rochester Diocesan Convention. It was an audience of over 600 and the stage was enormous. They were very welcoming and presented me with a sweet gift at the end.

It was odd arriving. The first time I'd been there was at least twenty years before when I was still a Pentecostal. Back then it was my church's annual convention which they called the *Bognor Bible Week*. The Rochester Convention took me mentally right back to it. What a different world it was then, and what a different God I believed in! I remember a world famous healing evangelist being there and doing his stuff, ridding people of their "spirits of nicotine" and "devils of fornication." At one point his microphone failed which some of us thought was the work of Satan and prayed against the demons that'd attacked the electrical circuits.

The Rochester people were easy to entertain. In fact some of the strongest reactions I've ever had occurred with them. Fiona, one of my stage volunteers, literally screamed as the moments of synchronicity unfolded in front of her. She shook like a leaf in the wind as she opened the envelope she'd been holding all along and revealed that the previously placed 10p piece had now transformed into the currency (and date) of the country and year she'd mentally chosen and "travelled back to" in time.

A new friend also came to meet me, a vicar who'd been through a very similar experience to me, though for a different reason. His crime was no crime at all. No, this cleric, who'd previously served as a kind and well thought of hospice chaplain for over a decade, was simply outed as a gay man by a malicious churchperson. He'd already been to see his bishop and confessed his sexuality a few years prior to that, and (as long as he promised not to draw attention to himself) he was told he could remain in post. But when outed it was a different matter. He had to go.

However he was not prepared to abandon his priesthood. He had served God and humanity for almost two decades and was not about to give up. In his mind he had been ordained as a priest of God not a priest of the Church of England. So, as someone with a passion for conducting rites of passage, he decided to set himself up as a freelance minister.

At the point when I met him he'd not heard from his hierarchy in three years and had been verbally attacked by many fellow clergy. He told me how he once visited his local cathedral for choral evensong and, as he left the church, the priest at the door looked him up and down and asked, "Why are *you* here?"

Shocked he simply replied, "I came to worship God."

"Why?" said the clergyman, coldly.

At that he left the building, sat down on a wall outside, held his head in his hands and wept.

I will never understand how far some so called Christians can stray in their attitudes from their own saviour's spirit of forgiveness and compassion. I've always said Jesus never seemed to have a problem with fallen humanity; it was hypocrisy he always found so hard to bear. This rejected priest told me how he holds families through their darkest times and how he feels most alive when doing so. The church may have rejected him but God certainly has not.

* * *

I've just done a meditation involving visualisation and something amazing happened. I found myself being mentally taken back to something I'd written a few years ago in my book *The Wizard's Gift*. In my imagination I *became* the main character Sam as he was led into a forest grove by the Wizard. I felt the strength and protection of the trees around me and the firm hand of the Wizard upon my shoulder. Then, quite out of the blue, the scene transfigured into my ordination as a priest. There I stood at the front of the cathedral surrounded by bishops and priests, all reaching out their hands of blessing towards me.

This brought a profound insight. I have been trying so hard to fit my new magical and Druidic awareness into my Christianity, but now I see it is the other way round.

I've been following magic ever since I was a boy. And my ordination ceremony (that took place about 15 years ago) was another step in my magical development, not a break with it. Church and the Christian priesthood is just one way of expressing and channeling the universal magic among many. It is a magical tradition and the sacraments are magical channels.

They (the Church of England) ordained me, which is a "making real of what already is." In other words they gave me their blessing and authority whilst also recognising what had already become evident in me naturally, my priesthood.

I am still a priest of God (a priest of the universal church) which is itself a fragment of the universal bond. The startling thing is that my ordination (still valid) adds something to my magic rather than vice versa. My hope, as I complete this year's diary, is that I will have come to a much clearer understanding of where I am within the realm of religious faith.

* * *

Something powerful strikes me as I return from the Rochester Convention at Bognor. This (freelance ecclesiastical ministry of mine) is what I'd always dreamed of. The fear and torment of the last few years was dreadful and I would not wish it on anyone, but the reward for "putting my money where my mouth is" and making my life authentic is priceless. I feel I could do this forever. I have almost nothing materially, yet inside I am discovering more riches each day.

I also know that the authenticity must continue. I must be on guard for temptations as I'm aware that I still have the capacity to be a "people pleaser." I could easily use the links I now have to become the church's magician and keep what I do safe and churchy. But I must not. I have to continue to be challenged myself and thus represent a challenge to others. I might be totally written off in a few months' time when my new book *The Path of the Blue Raven* is released. People will see more of me, and some of it they won't like. It might just be a little too much. If so then so be it.

* * *

Today I'm off to Liverpool. I'm on the train and just saw a mother weeping as she waved her young teenage son off on his next phase of army training, I'm sure part of her sorrow came from the inner nagging fear-filled question, "will I ever see my son again."

As I sit in the carriage I open a book, Richard Rohr's *Adam's Return*. It is a book of condensed wisdom from all his experiences of performing rites of passage for adult males. I had the privilege of being taken through such an experience by Fr. Richard in a

New Mexican desert in the year 2000. In some strange way it ties in with what I saw a moment ago, the young lad leaving his mum for the Army. The boy on the train and the weeping mother outside profoundly symbolise the major reason for native male initiation ceremonies. They were ancient puberty rites where boys left the security of their mothers and became men. I have found similar attempts to re-create such rites by certain Neopagan and Druidic authors. I will never forget my own initiation. For years I have wondered what effect the strange ceremony had on me but now, looking back, I can see quite clearly the strength it had given me. I doubt I would have ever had the courage to face my own demons in June 2007 and risk everything, were it not for the power of the initiation. It was as if I *had* to do it. Perhaps that's why I *have* to continue trying to walk this transformative pathway of self-honesty. A seed was sown during those two weeks in New Mexico which means I can never allow myself to be comfortable within the religious pretence of the so called respectable mainstream Christian world.

But where am I going now? And what is my faith now? I hope I have an answer to that question by the end of this book.

* * *

Liverpool was great. I stayed with my good friend Gerry. I hadn't seen him for over a year. My God has he been crapped upon from a great height and by the church again (though, this time, the Roman one) but that's another story. It was great to see him and spend some time in Liverpool, a really wonderful city. I was also taken to meet a Benedictine monk who lives in a wood as a hermit, and I witnessed the magical Chinese New Year celebrations in China Town (apparently one of the oldest Chinese communities in Europe). They sent sacred blessings of protection upon the shops as the firecrackers popped and the dragons danced.

* * *

For Druids, winter is the season when Mother Nature strips bare the trees of all their clothing, save for the symbolic evergreens. The woods and forests are then made up of millions of naked trunks, all huddled together for warmth. It is a powerfully symbolic time for stripping away, for shedding the old clothes that no longer fit or suit. January has been a month in which to try to remove some of the burdensome layers of my unnecessary baggage. I have tried to limit myself to fewer projects. For someone such as me, this is a hard task.

* * *

I have to admit to myself that the past month, whilst in many ways being fulfilling, has also been filled with a certain amount of spiritual confusion. I am following a Druidic course which is magnificent, and in many ways the Druidic community has become a new spiritual family for me. Yet I have also had the opportunity to take my magic deep into the Christian world. I have spoken and performed at huge Christian gatherings and conferences. I have performed Christian rituals that mark the passing of loved ones. I have visited many churches as a guest and even met a monk in a forest hermitage where I defended Anglicanism against his harsh criticisms of it. I have stayed as a guest of a Catholic priest and discussed the meaning of Jesus. I still feel strangely part of the Christian world, though I do not seem to be able to accept the whole package anymore.

* * *

The train takes me in the direction of home and gazing out of the window I see fields, trees and hedges rushing by. The land is something the Judaeo-Christian tradition often sees as a human possession. In our Holy Scriptures the first book, Genesis, contains the following words, "Fill the earth and subdue it." Does the earth really belong to us? How can it? Can Britain, for example, truly own the rock of Gibraltar when Britain itself has only existed for one second in comparison to that huge rock? A long time after the British have become but a distance memory, Gibraltar's rock will stand proud and strong at its location. My daughter once wisely pointed at the moon and said, "Daddy that's the same moon that the cave men would have seen." Her words sent shivers down my spine. How profound! She knew by intuition, a natural unlearnt wisdom, that the moon was the real permanence, not us, not frail humanity.

* * *

I've been considering my faith again. What, as a Christian with a Druidic heart, do I now make of the kind of religious questions I used to periodically ask myself? How would I answer them now? Let's have a go at answering the question I always began with:

Who is Jesus?

First of all, I believe Jesus to be both myth and history entwined. Jesus is a real human figure who existed literally at the time of the Roman occupation of Judea. He was a Jew who had a profound calling upon his life to challenge religiosity and make the divine accessible to all people, especially the disenfranchised, the marginalised and the poor. Truly he was a prophet and a radical. I do not believe he saw himself as God or The Son of God, but considered "sonship/daughtership of God" as something all people possess.

[At last I know what this book is for; it is a diary which will also completely revise a broken priest's Christian understanding and set forth a powerful vision of a practical spirituality that will be an encouragement for many others. It will be especially relevant for those who love the grace-filled insights and stories of Christ but cannot cope with

orthodox Christianity or the modern day established church].

Jesus knew instinctively that God (the Divine) was love, yet also that (ironically) religious institutions are most prone to blocking that very love and becoming barriers between it and the people rather than vessels. I am free to explore in a way I have not been for over twenty-five years. Unburdened and unfastened from the straightjacket of mainstream religion, I can now plunge into the river of spirituality outside churchianity.

The mythological side to Jesus is profound. As a myth, Jesus the son of God continues the long established theme of sun-gods who symbolise the natural cyclical pattern of life, death and re-birth.

For me perhaps Mary is easier to understand and apply in this way. As a literal human being she is the mother of the human Jesus, a special son with a prophetic gift. As a myth however she becomes another representation of the divine feminine, the goddess. I was always drawn to a statue in the church of All Saints, Hereford, a statue of mother and child. On many lunch breaks I would wander in, light a candle and say a Hail Mary. However I always felt a little uncomfortable with this. My natural Catholic heart needed this divine feminine figure, whereas my buttoned up Protestant head would shudder and snort out, "Popery."

Now I see her as another Venus, Aphrodite, Demeter or Bridgette; as another picture to add to the many mythic portrayals of the divine feminine. I can even light candles and send prayers to such mythical goddesses for they are fragments of the divine mosaic. I guess, therefore, I am still monotheistic, yet see the Oneness as something that is experienced in a multitude of ways all over the planet. It's like a bright sunbeam that can be split into a million independent rays of light, each one being transformed as it penetrates this culture or that religion and thus being changed by those cultures. Its source remains the same, though its end product is vastly different. The wonderful thing about the Pagan traditions is that their gods, goddesses, fairies and spirits represent every shade of human experience. Take Pan or Cernunnos for example; two of the horned gods of the Greek and Celtic cultures. They represent the tricky side of nature, of unpredictable forces; they are the forest gods and lords of the animal world, of earth, sensuality, touch, lust and life. No wonder many puritanical churchmen took one look at these goat-like green men and turned them into the devil.

* * *

The first month of the New Year is drawing to a close and, as it does, so I begin to recognise the synchronicities (moments of meaning-filled coincidence) that occur on an almost daily basis. Today I began reading the book my children gave me for Christmas. It's about Daemons. The first few pages made so much sense, as if I'd read them before.

I get very excited by the phenomenon of what some call "future memory." My own book *The Wizard's Gift* contained many examples of this. The thesis of *The Daemon* is that a higher (wiser) self exists in each one of us and that he/she knows the future because he/she has already lived it. How fascinating.

* * *

I've just spoken to someone I refer to as my "spiritual sounding board," a priest of the Birmingham Diocese. She was telling me about a particular pastoral ministry she's been involved with recently and how she was in a situation where she had to visit a Forward in Faith (anti women priest) church. Apparently the vicar of that church has been complained to because he'd allowed a woman priest inside his church.

What are we about? It's one thing to choose not to recognise such a ministry, but being offended because a woman priest stepped one foot inside the building? Where does that fit in with the Jesus who welcomed all? Is my friend more unclean than the fallen women or the tax collectors or the criminals who Jesus tenderly welcomed and raised back onto their feet? More and more I see Jesus as a corrector of religious mind set, not a founder of a new religion.

February

What a day! Snow greeted us this morning, a thick white blanket. It was beautiful. I always finish my magic shows by making a shower of snowflakes appear as I say the following words:

Did you know that a snowflake is a mirror? A tiny snowflake is a reflection of the human soul. If you really look at the leaf of ice that lands on your palm, you will see the creative design, the unique and beautiful pattern that is once only. It will never exist again in that form. It is perfect and precious as it is. It is like all other snowflakes, for it is made of the same substance, but it is unlike all others because it has its own special mark, like the finger prints on your hands. So, when you next see the first few flakes of winter snow don't just rush to thoughts of snowballs or stuck cars, think deeper. Think first of your own uniqueness and then the uniqueness of every other human soul. And thank God/dess for your place within this remarkable world-wide family.

* * *

I've just become godfather to my two little nieces. It was a lovely occasion but it prompted many questions; questions that I need to ask myself concerning what it is we're doing when we baptise. Is the terminology and symbolism really appropriate anymore? And are the services themselves relevant, dynamic, enchanting enough? It must be said (and I'm sure we all felt this) that the church service could have been brighter. To be symbolically plunging people into a radically new life and to be celebrating the beauty of the divine image within precious human souls ought to be a time for magic, wonder and joy surely?

* * *

This weekend I'm going to Leamington Spa to perform my magic at a parish church both on the Saturday afternoon and during the Sunday morning service. I'm so glad that some Anglican churches still occasionally use me like this. I still love the Church of England, no matter how much it drives me up the wall.

* * *

Today I visited an amazing woman; a spiritualist and shamanic healer. A few weeks ago we did an exchange, my book *The Wizard's Gift* for a set of her beautiful *Oracle Cards*. She invited me to her home to learn how to use them. The more I work with oracle and tarot cards, the more I see them as windows into the present moment of the sitter's life. I don't, therefore, regard them as a predictive tool for the future; more as a symbolic guide for the present. I guess I see the reading of them as the interpretation of randomness. There's nothing particularly special about the cards themselves in a mystical sense. One might just as easily find meaning when wandering through an art gallery and allowing the pictures to jog the mind or make synchronistic meaning. I see the tarot in the same way. They are a pile of interesting pictures that act as pictorial lessons to meditate on, which can indeed prompt, encourage, remind and even warn the sitter. But it is the sitter's own intuition and imagination (with the aid of reader) that actually imparts the knowledge. The cards simply help to uncover it.

* * *

Oh God, last week it was three. This week there are no less than *five* letters to the local press in today's paper, all concerning the *Ex-Vicar and the Pope* article. Some of them are anti and others are in support of what I said. What have I started?

* * *

It never ceases to amaze me what gentle inspiration comes from a simple morning walk. It becomes a meditative mantra, a natural pulse or a heart beat; a rhythm that stills the chattering mind and allows the rays of light to break through the usual storm clouds of the mind. We call it Awen in the Druid tradition, inspiration from above.

This morning my mind took me on a wonderful reflection of the ego. Oh how dominated we are by the manufactured self. The ego fears so much. It lives in fear. You can tell when someone is speaking/reacting purely from an ego level, for it will be dominated by fear. It manifests itself by self-protection, defensiveness, arrogance, hate and even violence.

Jesus came, not as a demi-god or supreme deity, but as a true spiritual master to pierce the ego with his metaphorical Zen-like master's rod.

We live most of our lives out of the ego. I am doing so right now as I write these words. My head is constantly talking:

"Will I meet the deadline?"
"What will they think of me if I don't?"
"It must be finished soon or else they'll never accept it."
"Will people hate me even more when they read my tattered story, and see how flawed I am?"

Feelings of guilt, fear, anger, defensiveness, ambition and so forth all come from the ego. Surrender, however, is the soul's way. Not the passive surrender of a coward who cannot stand up to bullies, but a deep strong and grounded surrender that says "reality is far better than pretence."

Reality shall set you free. Don't resist reality. Build what castles you can on solid ground, not illusions. To live like this of course causes pain and discomfort to ego but you are then on the road to true freedom. I am a very long way away from acquiring a genuinely free soul, but my facing the reality of my own sins, my own dirt and grime, is a step in the right direction.

* * *

It's strange. As I prayed at my altar today, I distinctly felt a natural awareness of a loving God/dess. Though Druidry tends to be polytheistic I still sense a universal loving presence which enfolds us. *Beautiful.*

I just heard the church bells. The building is about a mile away, but I can faintly hear the gong. If that building's anything it's a mixed blessing. I look at it and see a temple to God, a testament to faith, a remarkable symbolic and sacred space. Yet, I also see the tomb of God, a prison in which deity has become trapped within a tradition. A symbol of just about everything the founder of that tradition actually stood *against*. How ironic.

* * *

There's been more snow today. Money's been so short lately and I have a couple of weekend jobs that could easily bring in the equivalent of half a month's income, yet the snow could potentially rob me of this little comfort blanket. It's so tough finding work at the moment. The recession is real and what I do for a living (magic) is a luxury item, and the first to go in the financial cut backs. I have worked out what income I need each month. My breakeven is about a third of what I used to get as a vicar and these two shows could make half of that. I hope the snow doesn't spoil it. It makes me realise how nature dictates so much of our lives and how we are *not* in control. Snow, even for a Christmas-a-holic like me, has now become something to partially dread.

I'm walking in the country as I write this, and the picturesque landscape is startling and stunning. It's like a winter wonderland postcard image. God has laid a fluffy white blanket over it all, yet it is also a white blanket of death, a funeral shroud. The ancients feared this time of year. Our Celtic forebears saw it in terms of a divine struggle, a cosmic warfare, a fight between the gods. This battle is often depicted powerfully in Celtic ritual where the Lord of Midwinter fights with the Lord of Spring.

The coldness of my hands is making the pen hurt to hold. How excruciating it must have been for my own ancestors, this winter time of death. Indeed not just the Celts, but the people of the dark ages, the medievals, the Tudors and the Victorians too. We live in so much comfort and luxury here in the modern western world. All I face this weekend is not the loss of a limb to frostbite or the fear of being attacked by a winter predator in need of hot meat, but the potential loss of a few pounds and a sore pair of hands.

For the ancients, winter was a monstrously cold time of long dark nights, short days, fierce predators, lack of food and often literal death. That's why there are so many myths that surround the sun-god's re-entering of the situation in early spring. It was needed. It was what was going on in their lives. They *needed* the re-birth of the longer warmer days, literally.

And here we can see glimpses of the sun-god's warmth; snowdrops poking through the crisp white surface of the frosted ground; shoots of green popping up to herald spring. Welcome Spring Maiden, come gods of fertility and new life, come now Easter gods of hope and resurrection.

How our very own Christian traditions fit so neatly into this Pagan cultural landscape. Why did we end up cutting down an evergreen and placing it inside our homes? Why do we call our own resurrection festival Easter after the Norse goddess Eostre? All divine language is metaphor. It's how we express what we see, feel and experience as real.

* * *

I'm sitting in a huge charismatic Anglican church in Leamington Spa after staying the night with a sweet and friendly family of the congregation. I performed here yesterday afternoon and (though nervous due to the conservative evangelical tradition) was delighted by the response. They were so open, generous and "up for it."

Last night was wonderful too. Friends from the church joined us all and I entertained them with magic and mind reading. Later we discussed spiritual things and (bearing in mind their evangelical conservatism) the women amazed me by expressing how much they'd appreciated Peter Owen Jones and his *Around the World in 80 Faiths* documentary. They even loved his willingness to partake of the Wiccan ceremony! *They also fancied the arse off him.*

Now I'm sitting waiting to perform at a service where all the uniformed groups are on parade. How beautiful it was to walk into a church filled with the very high quality sounds of their music group. I really miss uniformed group services where all the boy-scouts, girl-guides, St. John's Ambulance and other organisations turn up with their banners and smart uniforms. I meant it this morning, when I said how much I miss them and always used to see them as the most enjoyable part of my role as a vicar. I always saw it as an immense privilege to have the church filled with the town's young people and their families, even if some of the more miserable members of the congregation didn't like their Sundays being interrupted by "strangers."

Today I'm preaching on my very favourite story of the Bible, the Prodigal Son or what I call *The Tale of Two Lost Sons*. To me this is the gospel in a nutshell and one of the most startling stories ever told. I never tire of hearing it. It still has the capacity to move me to tears. You can taste the emotional depth of the situation. You can feel the power of transforming grace penetrate the soul of the lost son as he melts in his father's welcoming arms.

But is it really a story about a lost son? Of course it *is* a story about a boy who loses himself. He runs away from home with half his dad's inheritance, wastes it all, falls flat on his face ending up spiritually and socially lost and later returns with the idea of becoming a servant. But I think of it more as a story about *two lost sons,* and when we start to see *two* lost son characters we begin to recognise *two* types of religious behaviour. Most people tend to see this story as a testimony of an evangelical repentance/ conversion, *yet it is so much more than that.* I believe that this story shows us the paradox between the person who does it all wrong and yet finds freedom and grace, and the person who does it all right and yet remains spiritually blind and unenlightened.

I also think that this story gives us a little insight into the unpopular theme of judgement. There are three main characters here; a father and his two sons. One of the two sons asks for his share of inheritance and leaves home. He leaves home because he wants to experience life. He certainly has all the security he needs with his father but that's clearly not enough. He seems bored and longs for stimulation. The father is *not* possessive. He does not cling to the boy pleading with him to stay. Neither does he allow himself to be offended and angrily send him off without his blessing. He simply *allows* him to leave. Thus the first deep insight into the nature of God comes right here at the very beginning of the story. God is not an over protective parent. He knows that for some of his children leaving home for a while is a necessary experience even if it ends in misery. Leaving home may well be leaving the religion that a young person's parents have struggled so hard to bring him or her up within. It is *any* experience that (in the end) teaches the seeker that what they are looking for cannot be found out there but is waiting back at home. The *irony* is that they would never find it *without* first going through the painful period of leaving home.

The journey made by the prodigal son is a quest for a

particular kind of life satisfaction where such life satisfaction can never be found. He sought adventure and stimulation, and for a while it was fun and gave a certain amount of pleasure but, like any compulsive behaviour, it cannot last *and will turn sour.* When his money ran out his luck also ran out, and so did his enjoyment of life. He soon discovered the consequences of looking for happiness in the wrong place. He began to suffer, but not because of any external judgement. The suffering was coming not from a wrathful father figure. His father was apparently still looking out, longingly searching the horizon with wide opens arms and grace-filled eyes. No, the boy's suffering was a direct consequence of his quest to find meaning in the wrong place.

Many Christians would assume that a person in this state was now well and truly under the judgement and wrath of God, especially considering he had not yet repented. But even if we study this story with care, we will not find *any* element of judgement in the father figure. All we see is a loving and forgiving dad waiting for his son to fall back into his arms.

The story says how the son "came to his senses," but it's important that we also recognise that he had actually assumed his father would not receive him back as a son. As the full reality of his predicament struck him, he suddenly remembered home, and the fact that life as a servant back there was so much better than life for him in the here and now. He knew what he would have to do, but expected no more than to be allowed to live as a servant (and perhaps he would not even be given that privilege).

He was ready to say to his father, "I am no longer fit to be called your son. Treat me as one of your hired workers." Clearly this boy *did not expect to receive forgiveness and a second chance.* One could even question whether he really *knew* his father's heart at all. He was imagining that his father was harbouring judgement and resentment against him. He was *projecting* his own self-judgement onto his father. I find this so interesting! Could it be that all "God-as-judge" language is a projection?

And, did the son repent at all? He certainly knew what words he would have to speak, "I have sinned against heaven and against you," but was this because he had really repented? One thing we *can* say is that the forgiveness (and I would say the *redemption*) was *already a flowing reality before* the son had a chance to get his words out. The normal evangelical understanding of a person receiving forgiveness/redemption is that it *follows* a person's repentance. The sinner turns and confesses his/her sin and in response, God forgives and thus redeems. But does it sometimes happen the other way round? Is our repentance sometimes a response to the redemption we have *already* freely received and experienced?

My own particular belief about this story is that it demonstrates God's totally unconditional love and forgiveness that flows ceaselessly in our direction. The son running into his father's arms was met by such mind-blowing grace and love that he melted. His repentance was in response to the redemption he was being offered. He had found what he *didn't even know he was looking for*, and certainly didn't expect to receive. He was indeed dead and alive again.

* * *

I'm now on the road again and on my way to another gig in Newent, Gloucester; a sixtieth birthday party. It was a great weekend and wonderful to be able to preach in a church again. As I spoke I was aware of my own place within the Christian world. In a sense I had played the role of the prodigal son myself when I went to see my "spiritual father" back in 2007 but, as my Catholic priest friend told me, he simply proved himself not to be my father at all. Yet in a strange way he has given me a gift. He has helped me to see where I belong and where I do not. I still have a ministry because I took that step. Had I remained within the church I would have suffocated and lost, if not my faith, then the integrity of my ministry. I do have a role, but it is outside the walls of the establishment now.

I am also reminded that deep down in my soul there still exists a notion of a God/dess of pure unconditional love and acceptance. That is who Jesus came to re-awaken in people, the freedom to know the God who breathes inside each one of us.

* * *

I woke up feeling rather low and disconnected today. I'm not sure why. My mind has become cluttered. I've been doing so much reading, networking, studying, forum posting and so on that I have unwittingly overloaded myself again. I'm confused and upset. It's a cycle. I tend to get into this kind of mess every so often. Too much of anything (even good things) can pollute the mind and create a lack of balance. *Consolidate* a word that comes up again and again for me.

God/dess where are you right now?

Mark, little brother, son, friend, I'm here.

Listen, I'm always near.

Always close, even within.

I am everything.

Listen to the happy songs of the feathered ones singing because they do.

I sing with them and through them.

Can you hear their countless tunes?

And there are other sounds that reflect my presence, other birds, ravens, yes I know you hear their distant croaks.

And even listen to the manufactured noise of the roads and sky, the sound of human travel, cars, lorries.

And further afield, above in the blue sky, the faint hum of an aircraft.

All human activity is part of my presence.

Look now Mark, what can you see?

The world around you hums and radiates the energy of my presences, from human creativity to natural animal life, to clouds up there above being blown on their way by the puff of my breath.

The Sun-God breaks through the clouds.

The grass, snow drops, and brown leafless trees, waiting to be re-clothed by Mother Nature's hands.

* * *

I am stunned. The book my children bought me for Christmas has not only rung bells for me, but one of my own books has rung similarly loud gongs in the head of its author Anthony Peake. The book I'm talking about is called *The Daemon*.

I've just received this letter from him:

Mark,

I have just finished reading The Wizard's Gift *and I am in a state of absolute amazement. Not only is it one of the best books I have ever read (and I must have read thousands in my life) but it is also stunningly prescient. You have written the novel to go with my* The Daemon. *I can now quite understand your excitement when your children bought you my book for Christmas. We have both travelled along very different paths but those paths have led to this point, at this time. It is clearly auspicious in some very important way. I am very excited that fate has worked in such a way, and I suppose that I am in no way surprised*

* * *

Oh my word, the local paper has had to add an extra letters page for the second week running. This week there are no less than *nine* letters about the whole homosexual clergy saga that I triggered with my article.

* * *

I'm having a country walk and I can hear a wonderful sound. Is it a woodpecker? How marvellous. It's cold, crisp, frosty and magical this morning. I love to hear the various sounds of the birds and other creatures. Last night, at twilight, I heard the pretty songs of the blackbirds. They sound like nightingales and are stunningly beautiful. They hold a powerful divinatory significance for Druids too. As a twilight animal, who sings at dawn and dusk, the blackbird is often seen as a bird of the boundaries between the two worlds, the physical world and other world (the land beyond where spirits roam). This is symbolised by the threshold between day and night where the birds sing the most eloquently.

Copcroft is my second favourite walking area, and I'm thoroughly enjoying being here this morning. Walking is a really great way of de-cluttering the mind and sifting/sorting out all the mess and confusion in the analytical head. This walk is a little hillier and makes me aware of how much I need to work on my own health.

Here I stand and suddenly I'm aware of how uncertain life is. There are the remnants of the last few snowmen over there, melting into the mud and grass. The field itself has not long been sown and the birds are pecking at the seeds and shoots. There's a clear pattern. Some skilled agriculturalists are able to read the signs of the seasons, but there is also a stark uncertainty about nature. The farmer is in control of the methods of his work but has to leave much of it to Mother Nature. We never really know what's around the corner. And maybe that in itself is a call to make the very most of the life we've been given.

* * *

I've been thinking about the "soul" today after a good friend asked me what my thoughts were. She's a priest and we often chat about spiritual things. This is how I replied:

Well I'm on unsteady ground here Caroline, probably heretical ground. I just don't accept the Judeo-Christian resurrection of the body teaching anymore. I remember being told I was quoting heresy back at theological college because I said I believe that the soul leaves the body at death, as if the person's essence somehow lives on. The guy said "no, that's the x,y,z, heresy and it has no place in orthodox Christianity." However I've always recognized a more Greek understanding in my own dealings with death. To me something does leave the body at death. I'm not sure what it is that leaves but when I see a dead person it seems like something is missing. I think the something missing is what we call the soul. But what is it? What is the soul? I'm coming to believe that the soul is the true YOU, the YOU that is there before and after your birth and death, the YOU that is the hidden observer of your life, the essence of your essential Self. I think it's closely related to what I called the Divine-Me in *The Gospel of Falling Down* and the Inner Wizard in *The Wizard's Gift*. It's possibly also related to what the Gnostics called the Daemon. They had a name for the *Little-Me* too, the Eidolon.

* * *

February is a dark and cold month. I feel like a curry tonight to warm me up. Why are all the best things so bad for you? Shove Tuesday is coming soon and I've been invited to lead a clergy quiet day in Birmingham. I'm going to use *The Gospel of Falling Down* to guide them on some thoughts about failure and grace.

* * *

Wow, I've just seen the cover for my new book *The Path of the Blue Raven - from Religion to Re-enchantment.* It's stunning. My first idea was to use a stunning oil painting by the American artist Ragen. Her picture of a woman's profile with a raven formed out of her hair is wonderful. However my publisher decided against it on the grounds that it looked more like the cover of an erotic fantasy novel than a real life story. Then I came across a photograph of a raven flying through a dark forest, the blue sky in the horizon as a sign of being led out of a dark place into the light. It suited the book's theme perfectly, and the designer did his stuff. The result is a wonder to behold. Now whenever I look at this book I will see my own raven spirit-guide leading me into the light and onto the next stage of my journey. It's been an adventure where much of what I've previously written about has been worked through. For example *The Gospel of Falling Down* enables people to find their true (beautiful) selves through the transformative experience of failure. I have suffered from much failure but (as the years have passed) have learned to fear it less and see it more as a necessary tutor rather than a foe to be avoided. Failure is part of a normal, healthy, authentic human life. If we say no to failure we say no to humanity. Darkness is a necessary part of finding light. My own darkness is as much an ingredient of my own salvation as my light.

* * *

Some of the letters to the local press (sparked off by my *Ex-Vicar and the Pope* article) have amazed me by their own total misconception of the spiritual/human quest. One of them states that "God cannot look upon darkness, and cannot even look upon those who sin." What planet are these people on? Have they forgotten what the Christian faith was about at the very beginning? The whole thrust of the Christ story subverts the purity code culture and says God's in the shit, in the mess and muddle. Christ symbolises a God that embraces darkness, evil, sin and real humanity at its most human. Jesus, if we see him as the human face of God, resisted and ignored the religious customs and the strict purity obsessions. He plunged right into the murky and mixed humanity of his day, mingling with the so called gluttons and sinners, tax collectors and prostitutes, and getting a name for it in the process. He didn't care a damn about what we call "respectability." I imagine that if Jesus could be sent 2,000 years into his future (via some sci-fi Tardis-type machine) and if he stumbled across the equivalent type of people and places pointing out that the kingdom of God is within them he'd have more than letters written to the press about him. I imagine the poor dude would be locked up, or worse. Wake up. Jesus Christ *means* that God mixes with mess, muddle, shit and darkness. In fact it's how he can transfigure it. He does not come to judge, condemn or send folk to hell, but to hold, heal, bless, touch and make meaning out of the mess and muddle. We need gods who are real, human, incarnate, undetached, earthy and thus able to cope with you as you are and me as I am.

* * *

As a very emotional and heart dominated person I feel that one reason why I am clinging on to the remnants of my Christian past is that I still need the Christ-as-Lover archetype. The magical Pagan path really speaks to me and makes sense right now, yet I still need that God-as-Unconditional-Lover attribute in my picture of the Divine. Of course I have to be honest and say that Unconditional love is something the church often talks about yet fails to model. My own experience of Christianity has tended to be a lack of love and more emphasis on judgement.

In his latest episode Peter Owen Jones met an amazing god

down a mine in Brazil called "El Tio." He has three enormous horns, one of them being the huge erection between his legs. The Catholics see him as the devil but his worshippers do not. He is in fact a very typical horned god, in the same sense that the Greek Pan or the Celtic Cernunnos are. There are many such nature spirits and horned gods within global indigenous religions. They symbolise the earth, the wildness of nature, sacrifice and re-birth and raw masculine energy. They are both friendly and fierce. They are untamed like C.S. Lewis's Aslan. On the same episode Peter also visited the shrine of an amazing "punk" virgin Mary called "Sante Morte," the saint of death. She seems to be able to offer something to those who feel worn down, imperfect and neglected by official Christianity. The church has lost a lot of respect and allegiance by setting up huge barriers between God and man. This saint comes right into the grasp of the downtrodden, offering a realistic, human and relevant message of hope.

On this subject I am beginning to see how (ironically) the religions that seek to foster and promote "purity" and "perfection" and the "God of light" are the most prone to what they themselves term "darkness" because of their tendency to avoid confronting it in themselves and the habit of projecting such "evil" onto others out there, people whom they fear or simply don't understand. Thus Christianity ends up with the devil because it cannot cope with the human, the base, the instinctual and often erotic nature of humankind. Nature-based paths have gods who can hold this brute force of nature and make sense of it. There is a more optimistic and sympathetic approach to and acceptance of humanity because they don't separate the spiritual from the physical.

Christianity should really be non-dualistic, yet it became one of the most terrifying of all the dualistic faiths. Jesus faced his own darkness (devil) in the desert not so we don't have to, but to encourage us to all face our own inner demons. Jesus did not play the avoidance game. He recognised the presence of what we call darkness (the shadow) within. This is why I think Jesus still has a spiritual relevance in our world today.

* * *

I saw ravens at my mother's house yesterday. The familiar sound jolted me and there they were, doing acrobatics like a stunt plane allowing itself to free fall.

* * *

It was always my goal to have no ulterior motives as a priest within the community. By that I mean no hidden intentions that others would later realise were the main reason for my presence within a particular situation. In my opinion I should be a friend to the neighbourhood/community, embrace people as they are and have no hidden intentions to convert or talk about church.

I remember a case when I was in the local pub and we were evangelised by a whole gang of Born Again Christians. It was Christmas and the whole episode was cringe making. The pub was buzzing and the atmosphere was electric. I was (unusually) wearing a dog collar as I'd been on a previous religious function. Everyone knew me and everyone trusted me. I was the vicar and I was a friend. I was not there to push my religion, but was obviously available should anyone wish to talk about faith matters or life in general. In fact, to be very honest, my main purpose for being there was because I *need* friends and a pint or two as much as anyone.

Then it happened. The doors burst open and in came a crowd of about half a dozen guitar carrying carol singers. The fact that they shouted "okay, we're gonna sing you some carols" was bad enough, but the handing out of religious literature was just appalling. They could have come in, gone to the bar and asked permission to sing. Then (after delighting everyone) they could have quietly left. It would have perhaps been seen as a little Christmas gift from some local Christians. But as it happened they came, they preached and they left their rubbish. *They were full of ulterior motives.* Little did they know that only a week earlier I'd conducted a short, simple and informal carol service in that very pub because I was invited to by the landlady.

I was reminded of this today because I've heard that there are a few within the Christian-Pagan world who have similarly ulterior motives. They befriend Pagans and infiltrate their communities on the grounds that they are also Pagans but then (once they've gained trust) try to convert them. I find this an abuse of friendship and abhorrent. True friendship is not about squeezing people into your own mould; it's about love and acceptance of people for who they already are.

* * *

The Eleventh (or third) Commandment - Be Your *True* Self.

I am honestly not trying to be facetious here, and I am certainly not seriously attempting to re-write the Jewish Ten Commandments or the Christian Two Commandments (love God and love your neighbour as yourself). However none of us can keep these rules constantly, no matter how religious we are or how hard we try. They are certainly a sensible guide for life, but humankind (with human weaknesses) simply cannot achieve perfection and, ironically, it is those who struggle and strive to be ritually pure and morally perfect who often end up the most hateful and un-Christ-like of all. They may not murder, commit adultery or even masturbate but boy do they suffer from other "sins" like pride, superiority, intolerance and a supreme lack of hospitality to the very folk who the original Jesus seemed to make good buddies of (tax collectors, prostitutes, sinners).

Projection is the psychological phenomenon where people,

who cannot consciously recognise their own self-hatred, subconsciously choose scapegoat figures on whom to dump all their self-disgust and intolerance. State religion has of course a callous past history of such projection on a mass scale. Just think of the thousands of witches (practitioners of the old ways, herbalists and midwives) who lost their lives across Europe in such acts of projected hatred. A more modern example is of course the homosexual "witch-hunts." These souls may not be subject to the ordeals of the literal witch-hunts but they certainly experience being metaphorically burned at the stake. Reality shall set you free. Truth about self and truth about neighbour has to be real truth. Such truth can, however, cost you everything of course (as I have discovered).

Truth is about self-awareness and self-honesty. It's about recognising the flaws, the wounds, the cracks within and being honest about them. Nevertheless the church suffers from a compulsion to paper over the cracks. For God's sake Christianity was always *about* the cracks. The Man himself wandered around bumping into one broken person after another; and what do all broken people have in common? Cracks. As Leonard Cohen sang, "it's how the light gets in."

Cracks. We don't like them but boy do we need them. Don't deny them. Don't try and fill them in with metaphorical wood sealant or putty. It won't last and, worse, it will grow gangrenous. Rather, let them be seen and let the truth they point to enlighten us. It won't be pleasant at first but will surely lead to more grace than covering them up ever could. Let them see the fresh air where they can heal.

A reading from the book of St. Pretentious:

And Jesus spoke unto the sinner before him saying, "Shhhh. You don't know who might be listening? Better you hide yourself away for a while and pretend nothing's happened, than tell the truth and rely on mercy."

"I beg your pardon," said the sinner.

"Well, you know what people are like round here," said the Lord, "and while we're at it don't, for God's sake, bring my name up when people ask you what happened. I've got enough problems round here without being associated with the likes of you. Do you get me?"

* * *

I had a chat with the manager of a small Mind Body Spirit store yesterday. He had just had a customer totally embarrass him by dishing out unwanted and unasked for "spiritual" advice. My emphasis of "spiritual" is tongue in cheek, because such advice is usually about as genuinely spiritual as an Elvis mirror is genuine art. For some reason the "spiritual world" seems to breed a lot of people who think they can speak *for* God (or angels etc.) and who see it as their divine duty to force their opinions on others. I do understand that many of them genuinely feel they're helping, but what's wrong with a listening ear or a sympathetic hug? I have found them both within the world of Christian spirituality as well as the so called New Age movement; people who know all the answers and never stop displaying them, even when no one's asking any questions.

We should stop taking ourselves so seriously! The Universe is approximately 16 billion years old. We, the human species, have literally just arrived on the scene. Who are we to think we know anything?

When I was a vicar one of the biggest causes of my constant grief was the handful of "super spiritual" parishioners whose vocation was to pester their priest with daily doses of sanctimonious "God talk." They came from all the major Church of England traditions. There was the Anglo-Catholic (almost nun-like) pious old woman who tried to model herself on her own spiritual heroine, yet often failed to give off any Christ-like warmth or acceptance. She was so concerned with what was "right" that she came across as legalistic and cold. Yet she did have a genuinely deep love for God and often surprised me by how that "lovely old woman" inside her would (occasionally) break through.

There was also the evangelical equivalent, a man with a mission from God (a right pain in the arse to be honest). He'd bombarded the last half dozen clergy with his "calling," and even written to every bishop in the Church of England about it. God had given him this mission and no darn cleric was going to get in his way. No matter how many of us tried to explain he just couldn't see that, while his idea was a good one, it was already being done. In his own way he was a nice man but was about as interesting and up to date as an Ovaltine advert, yet he swore that he was the one to take the gospel to the *real* people of the world outside the church.

* * *

I just bumped into a good old clergy friend after doing a funeral at Hereford Crematorium. He's a great guy and a vicar who's managed to keep hold of his own persona and not be moulded into the clerical stereotype you occasionally come across. He told me how he'd been more and more convinced by the non-realist argument for a God-free faith.

When I first started training for ministry there seemed to be much more variety allowed. I was put on a pre-college course called *The Aston Training Scheme* where anything and everything was experienced. My fear is that, today, such freedom does not exist. There were many non-realist members of my theological course and they were not demanded to conform. Now such people are often driven out or not allowed a foot through the vocational door in the first place.

I've always believed that the beauty of the Anglican approach is that it has an ability to hold together, under one umbrella, all the many sects, traditions, divisions of the church. Many people (most people in fact) change their opinions and perspectives on a weekly or monthly basis. Some need to go through serious bouts of doubting in order to come out the other side with a faith strong and secure and worth fighting for.

Others taste non-realist ideas and stay there. In a fashion it is a Buddhist way of being a Christian. I'm not a non-realist myself however. I still believe and (I think) experience, the *real* presence of the Divine.

* * *

I'm at Blackpool Magic Convention sitting in an auditorium with a huge audience of magicians. It's a stage interview with two of my mentor/teachers, Jeff McBride and Eugene Burger. They are incredible people who have injected huge doses of spiritual enthusiasm into their art which, in turn, breathes life into others. These two, representing the high energy sorcerer/stand up magician (Jeff) and the wise man/sage (Eugene), represent how to live a fully magical life.

Their philosophy is bewitching. They have helped me in my quest to bring a spirituality and sense of meaning into my own magic. As time goes by I am more and more aware of how the various strands in the web of my life are slowly being drawn together and woven into a threefold rope:

The Magical (both illusion magic and real magic)
The Religious/Spiritual (both Christian priesthood and Druidic)
The Artistic (writing, drawing/painting and music making)

Stage magic is a vocation. A good magician reaches out with metaphorical wand and touches the latent magic buried deep down in the spectator's soul, so they cease to be a spectator and become a co-creator. This is very similar to how I see priesthood. A true priest is one who awakens and enables the priesthood of all those whom he or she ministers among. The trouble is that both magicians and priests often see their vocation as one of "I can do what you cannot do for yourselves" whereas I would say that I am a magician *because* everyone is essentially a magician and I am a priest *because* everyone is essentially a priest.

* * *

It's Monday morning and I'm now on the train home. It's 10.45am. I got in about 6am this morning after a whole night with Jeff, Eugene and the enchanting British magician Romany. Jeff amazed me by thanking me for a playing card effect I shared with him about three years ago. Romany calls it my *Priest's Revenge* trick. It employs a deck of cards known as a cheek to cheek deck and Jeff said "I do cheek to cheek because of you. You are a very creative guy. Keep it up." I left for bed feeling honoured and encouraged.

* * *

Tomorrow I'm off to visit a clergy chapter in Birmingham to talk about failure and grace, my pet theme. I learn so much from getting things wrong. There is a kind of karmic consequence to all our actions, good or bad. This is one central teaching within all the magical traditions; a biblical equivalent is "you reap what you sow."

* * *

I'm in the middle of leading the clergy quiet day and just had some comments that warmed my heart and made me realise that I must keep offering this stuff to the Christian world. People are so tied up with guilt and pain, and it's amazing how my retreat frees people to talk of their experiences in an open and liberated way.

My Gosh, the grief and misery people live with. And bullied clergy too! I come across so many of them while leading these quiet days. I often have the privilege of being listener to a great deal of expressed pain on these days, and today is no exception. We closed with a celebration of the Eucharist and my being part of it didn't feel odd or awkward at all. In actual fact I felt quite at home.

* * *

Today I took my beautiful children to the safari park. I really needed it. It was heaven to be with them both and enjoy the amazing animals together, even though we were peed on from above by a giant fruit bat!

* * *

Today there are more financial worries; the mortgage this time. I need to find £2,500 from somewhere *and fast*. There goes a holiday for yet another year. Sometimes it's so hard. Yet gold is often found in the gutter. Magic is discovered in the mess. Pure wisdom is stumbled across in the pain and worry of life. I just had a wonderful thought enter my head. I suddenly became aware that I have actually found what I've always been searching for, a spiritual way of life that is both mystical yet also liberal. I could never find that within mainstream Christianity but the Neo-pagan/Christian mix has given me exactly that, an open, liberal (even intellectual) faith, yet saturated by lashings of magic and mystery.

* * *

Today I met a sweet couple who live in an idyllic spot in South

Herefordshire; heaven really. They've invited me to help them prepare and celebrate their baby's naming ceremony. They explained what they're looking for and, yes, I know I'm the right person. I don't wish to sound big headed but I can't think of anyone else around here that'd be able to do what they want. They're looking for an experienced officiant who has a good grasp of nature-based paths and who can help them construct a beautiful eclectic ceremony that celebrates the elements and is able to give thanks to the Universe for their little boy.

March

I'm travelling to Leicester and Coventry to lecture at the Magical Societies of both cities. Then I return for a funeral. That's all I have on for the rest of the month so far (apart from one private unpaid event at the very end of the month). Sometimes I honestly don't know how my family and I survive. I struggled enough financially as a parish priest but this is living on a shoestring.

This came to me as a whisper while I drove my car:

Mark, trust, don't worry, all will be well, hang in there, everything belongs.

* * *

I'm now sitting in the hotel bar after having just done the first of my two lectures and I feel bad because, though I gave it my best, I know I didn't really connect with the audience. I could have done better. I need to really work on this.

Failure, it cracks open the ego's shell and bloody hurts, as any experience of breaking does. But then, if we look inside the cracks we can find the hidden answers we need so badly. We will learn lessons for the future. We will be better off for it.

Failure, it feels like sinking into the mire of hopelessness; yet under it is a rock, a solid rock where we can stand and begin the re-building process.

* * *

I'm now on my way to the second magic lecture in Coventry. This morning I had a few hours to kill before setting off, so I walked into Leicester city centre. As always I managed to find a large bookstore in which to waste some time. There I had one of those moments that could only be described as synchronistic. I was browsing the shelves in the enormous Mind Body Spirit area and I noticed the spine of a book that slightly jutted forward. It seemed to have an aura and sat there gently throbbing and shimmering and willing me to pick it up.

So I did!

It was by an author I'd not come across before called Gill Edwards and the book was called *Wild Love*. I knew I had to buy it. I walked back to my hotel, found a quiet place to sit and began reading. Within minutes I knew I was looking at the words of a kindred spirit, someone who'd been through much pain and was still living in a situation of emotional trauma, yet had managed to find peace. In essence it was a book that encouraged people to be authentic. From those moments I knew for certain that this book and author were going to have a huge impact.

* * *

I'm now in my room after having opened another book I've been reading lately, my daily prayer book. Talk about synchronicity. Today's prayer from Tess Ward's extraordinary book *The Celtic Wheel of the Year* sums up everything I've been feeling, especially regarding the sense of failure at last night's lecture.

She writes:

Praise to you who knows our harsh times,
When the universe withdraws its friendliness,
And we are thrown back on our own resources.
For whether we feel your absence or presence
There can be no pretence.
Praise to you who bears our 'how long?'

Tess's whole Office for Tuesdays in March is an astonishing piece of liturgical magic that breathes courage into the frail and fractured clay of my life.

* * *

I'm back home again and walking in *The Grange*. A blanket of frost decorates the area this morning. Birds are in full voice. It's gorgeous. Blue crocuses poke their heads above the cold earth's crust. This is just what I need to soothe my aching head.

I'd just had a phone chat with my rather volatile friend and at one point I said that responding to unkindness in a like for like manner does not help, but blessing those who hurt you is a far better way than cursing. Quite understandably he replied, "Oh yeah. And look just where it's got you!"

In my imagination I looked and saw my ransacked house, lack of money, letters of hate, behind the scenes bullying and ever continuous grappling with the results of June 2007, *and I could clearly see what he meant.* Yet, there is another perspective to the situation. When I really stand back and look out at the landscape, I can see freedom, open gates, blue skies, rainbows and pots of gold. I can see that my own way, though I lost an idyllic lifestyle and a good job, has in fact brought true freedom, and that is priceless.

And this freedom is not just for me. It's a gift for those closest to me too because I am essentially much happier and far less weighed down now. I no longer live in an ecclesiastical prison cell. I am true to myself now; the Truth has set me free.

* * *

Lately there have been some heated discussions on various web forums about magic (not stage magic but *real* magic) and its potential dangers. I am well aware of the many pitfalls of magic and the occult but I do feel that the human psyche has much power in this area. I'm not sure yet how to differentiate between actual external psychic influences and those of the human mind. I feel very comfortable with Druid chief Philip Carr Gomm's very grounded and sensible approach. Druidry seems to have a very natural approach to magic.

Whereas many forms of Paganism believe in and openly practise the magic of rituals, prayers and spells to effect actual change, it is very hard to find Druidic books on ritual magic or spellcraft. You can find them if you look hard enough, but even when you do there seems to be a more cautious approach. For many modern Druids magic is what life is, and to be fully immersed or plugged in to the flowing energy of life on this enchanted planet is how living a magical life is understood. It is less to do with forcing actual changes and more about soaking up the magic of what already is. So the magic of transformation is about the transforming of the person needing the magic, rather than his or her material situation. What is often needed is not a new situation but a new way of perceiving it. This is where it ties in with Christian prayer. Is petitionary prayer to do with trans-forming a situation and solving a problem by changing actual circumstances or is it more to do with changing the praying person's perspective? It's possibly a both-and, but I tend towards the latter. I feel that to pray through a difficult problem helps the praying person come to his or her own conclusions about how to deal with the problem. The actual problem will seldom go away but a new way of looking at it might lessen the power of the problem in that person's life.

I'm not saying that praying for actual change is in any way unnatural (such compulsions are very natural, and sometimes miracles do seem to occur) but in my experience the prayer of surrender to a situation often yields a more healthy result than to try and force change which, when it refuses to come, causes more misery. It is the difference between saying that "you can *have* what you *want*," or "you can learn to *want* what you *have*."

With reference to supernatural magic and spellcraft I've come across many Druidic authors who say they do not believe in supernatural magic at all, because magic is simply *part* of nature; magic is therefore *totally* natural. And with reference to spellcraft there is a healthy respect among Druidic authors (and other Paganisms) for this potential power and, even, a caution with regard to any attempt to manipulate actual change.

* * *

I've been reading Scott Cunningham's bestselling book *Wicca: A Guide for the Solitary Practitioner*. My initial reaction is *oh how beautiful*. His portrait of a Wiccan landscape is profoundly enticing. The God and Goddess are loving, yet earthy, and exist within all things. They are immanent as well as transcendent. I really warm to this, though I'm still not sure about magic as spellcraft. Something still unnerves me about the notion of manipulating change by will and ritual. Then again, what do we Christians do when we beg God for miracles?

* * *

I'm on my way to Sheffield. I have a lunch time magic show for the Student's Union at the University. How cool. I've just taken the wrong turning though, resulting in a 20 mile detour down two different motorways.

Wrong turns. Our life is full of them, and how frustrating they are. How wasteful they seem, yet they often quite unexpectedly turn out to be necessary. When we go the wrong way and discover we're travelling in the wrong direction we have to stop, and stopping is so important for life, for living a fully connected and soulful life. Sometimes the only time we actually stop is when necessity demands it. I guess the enlightened life is one where such necessary knee jerk halts become less necessary.

* * *

Oh well, yet again I've proved myself to be one of the world's biggest idiots! It's about 9.30am. I've just arrived at the Student Union block of Sheffield Uni and, fool that I am, have discovered that my 11.30am -1.30pm gig is actually supposed to be from 11.30pm until 1.30 in the morning. I've arrived 14 hours early!

I don't know whether to laugh or cry. It's my birthday and something special had been planned for me. Oh well it's my fault. I may as well try and get some sleep.

[I can never sleep in a car in daylight].

I'm starting to feel very sad about this now. How do you kill 14 hours in a town you don't know, dressed up as a magician and already worn out because of the 5am start? I guess I'd better try to make the most of it. Perhaps I can find a University porter to get me a room to write in and use the time constructively.

* * *

Those lovely porters. I told them my plight and they took pity and let me crash in their staff room. I popped down to the café and bought a little food and a drink, and then (for the second time) tried to shut my eyes for a while. Again, no luck. No luck writing either. The muse has left me. So I've now decided to walk into town.

This is turning out to a long and frustrating day. I've just wandered into town and hope I can manage to get some sleep later; otherwise it's going to be an agonising drive home.

I found the city centre and spent an hour in Waterstones. I had the strangest feeling while I was there, as if I was *supposed* to be there. I'm now sipping an Americano with milk in a coffee bar. It's only 4pm and I'm not on until 11.30!

I have a funny feeling about all this. When I was in Waterstones I started asking myself, "What if all this was for a purpose?" I'm feeling tired and fed up but I have the distinct feeling that I'm going to end up thanking God/dess that I came to Sheffield too early.

* * *

Sheffield city centre is very elegant. The pedestrianised area is smart, clean and relatively peaceful. It's quite busy too, even within a recession.

I still have a feeling that I should be here. Now it's beginning to direct me, the inner feeling. I have a deep down urge to get up and walk back out into the town square and continue down to the left, into the major part of the city. Something awaits me. I feel the inner wizard stirring. He wants to show me something again. I'm ready big brother. Teach me. I'm open.

Mark, find the cathedral. I have something to show you. And you're going to weep when you see it!

I have no idea where the cathedral is, or even if there is one.

Come, follow me!

I followed the voice out into the street, the busy town centre. I could see a few ecclesiastical looking buildings but only one was actually a place of worship, and it was certainly not a cathedral. The others were just important town buildings. But I decided to follow my inner instructions and walk *left* and down to the bottom of the pedestrianised area.

I reached the bottom. It was only a couple of hundred yards from where I was having coffee. There were some large buildings all the way down either side of the broad street. I stood at the bottom and then saw what had been previously hidden.

Sure enough, just to the left, across a road was the cathedral. My heart leapt. Part of my head had being telling myself how ridiculous this whole thing was whereas a different, deeper, part of me was gently "shhhhhhh-ing" the conflict and quietly reassuring me that I would find it. So I was both amazed and at the same time unsurprised.

I hurried across and walked into a full blown festival Eucharist. The sidesman on the door said, "Have you come for the service?"

Well by that point I knew I had. "Yes," I replied as he handed me a service book. He said "Oh, how lovely." It made me feel so welcome.

I sat down at the back of the huge church, *and wept*. The music, the choir, the women priests at the altar, the ambiance, the presence, the welcome and the feeling of being at home totally melted me.

Now I know why I came to Sheffield early. God/dess spoke too, not audibly but in my heart. Deep down I felt an assurance and, if this could be put into words, they would have been the following, *Mark I've not finished with you yet, within this context.*

I now know that I'm still a priest and that I must not give up my Christian priesthood too quickly. I spoke to the minister on duty and told him some of my story. He said, "Once a priest always a priest."

From where I'm now sat I can see a beautiful little chapel and there's no one between it and me. It's inviting me. It's beckoning me forward. Could it be saying that there is a future for me even within the church's ministry after all? I can see myself kneeling at the altar again, with a bishop blessing me and welcoming me home, but *as I am* with all I've learned from being in such different places.

I am in shock!

* * *

I cried buckets in that place. I was back in my original spiritual home and I felt all the pain and anguish of the demand for my resignation, yet also love, compassion, healing and warmth from the great God/dess:

Mark you will never forget today! It will change your life. The future has taken a new direction.

And all because I arrived here too early.

Yes. Everything belongs!

* * *

So what did that cathedral experience do for me now I've had a little time to reflect?

1 Brought back memories, happy and painful ones.
2 Evoked feelings of an all-embracing God again, a motherly/fatherly God/dess who welcomes, heals, forgives and makes use of the broken.
3 Renewed a sense of my priestly vocation.
4 Enabled me to cry, cry and cry in God's house; to let go and receive the healing love of God/dess. I can see this God/dess in all things.
5 Gave me another encounter of Jesus! He was there. He is a God-image. He is a God! His literal self may have been a wise man and 100 per cent human, but his mythic self became a deity.

His lessons are:

Love. You are loved as you are.

Healing. You can be healed of inner pain if you learn to accept yourself.

Brokenness is where the God-light shines. The marginalised are the ones who can see the truest image of God for they are empty of self. They are at the place where there's nothing more to cling to and nothing to protect. The need for the beginner's mind is clear within the wisdom teaching of Jesus.

* * *

I'm now sitting in a delightful Indian restaurant, still in Sheffield. The waiters are charming. I am waiting for my chicken tikka dansak and enjoying an ice cold Cobra shandy on the table in front of me. I'm completely in awe of the experience that just happened. I see it as a new lesson from the Divine-Me.

I would not now change today. If I could I would not go back in time and make sure I read the agent's booking form correctly. No, this was all meant to be. The Spirit certainly does move in mysterious ways.

This all reminds me of a strange experience I once had hitch-hiking in Northern Israel. I was a teenager at the time and was enjoying a few months on a kibbutz. In fact enjoying is not really the right word to use at all. It was a gruelling experience; the hardest manual work I've ever had to do in my life. We were woken up at 4am each morning, to be driven down into the cotton fields in the valley below for three hours' work *before* breakfast. The days were long and hot. We spent hours out in the fierce sun and, on top of that, there was the ever constant threat of terrorist attacks. Only a few years before my visit, two gunmen had forced entry and killed a man and his children at the same kibbutz. In fact while I was there an armed gang were captured trying to get in. Everyone there had a gun and the sound of bombing and gunfire was a daily occurrence. The most frightening night of the four months was when it was my turn to work through the night driving a tractor at walking pace for the others to wind in all the irrigation pipes. It had to be done in the night because the ground was moist and the pipes could be freed more easily. However we'd been told that one of the techniques used by terrorists was to silently fly hang-gliders over the valleys, dropping explosives. And there I was, sat in the tractor, lit up like a firefly within a sea of darkness. A sitting duck, terrified.

In many ways it was my growing sense of dissatisfaction and

disenchantment with Christianity (then of the Pentecostal variety) that motivated my trip. I wanted to go back to the place where it all began and experience the land of Jesus first-hand. I was a teenager back then and the Israeli Palestinian political situation was not something I'd been able to fully get my head round. I'd heard strong arguments on both sides and I guess I could see both points of view.

However the connection between my experience in Sheffield Cathedral and my time in Israel was not to do with the politics of the land or with my fear of being caught up in the conflict, but with a strange encounter of hitch-hiking. Before leaving the UK I was told of a Galilean fellowship of Messianic Jews (Jewish believers in Jesus as Messiah) who welcome non-Jewish believers to worship among them. I was also given the name of a couple who worship there and who might be willing to take me if I were to get in touch with them. Their names were Benny and Naomi. The only problem was that I was based on a kibbutz right up in hills on the most northerly border of Israel and Lebanon; whereas the fellowship met near the Lake of Galilee which was about twenty-five miles south (maybe more). Benny and Naomi could take me (if I got in touch with them) but even they lived quite a distance away from me down in the town of Kiryat Shmona.

I'd been living on the kibbutz a few weeks when I really started craving some kind of spiritual fellowship so I looked for Benny and Naomi's details and realised, to my dismay, that I'd lost them. I thus gave up any hope of attending a fellowship while out there. Even if I could find the details of the fellowship there was no way of getting there by myself because the other problem was that (being Israel) everything stopped on the Shabbat, so there was no public transport. And, being a Messianic fellowship, it met on the Shabbat rather than the Sunday for worship. In fact most churches met on the Shabbat.

Then, one afternoon, I'd managed to get a lift down into the town of Kiryat Shmona for a wander round and a treat of a falafel or two. A few hours of wandering the streets had become one of my greatest pleasures, though getting back was always a chore because it was such a long walk back up the hill to the kibbutz. I never hitch-hiked because I've always considered it to be a particularly unsafe practise, and here there was the added threat of being in an area of conflict.

So I started walking back up the hill and, after a while, noticed the sound of a car driving behind me. I thought about it and decided to trust my instinct, so I stuck out a hand. The car stopped and the driver asked me where I was going. On learning that my destination was the same as theirs they offered me a lift. They were a middle-aged couple and the woman told me they never picked up hitch-hikers, but that they'd both felt the urge to stop and offer me a lift. I asked them where they were from and they told me they lived in Kiryat Shmona. Apparently they made the trip up to the kibbutz where I was staying once a month to teach singing lessons.

Then a thought came to my head and I found myself asking the following (rather foolish) question: "Look I know this might sound like a crazy thing to ask, especially considering the population of Kiryat Shmona [it's about 23,000], but I was given the name of some people before I left the UK, a couple who may be able to take me somewhere I'd very much like to go. I don't suppose, by any chance, that you know them? Their names are Benny and Naomi."

At that the woman span round in her seat, "Oh my, I'm Naomi," she said, and pointing to the driver, continued, "and this is Benny." As we talked we all realised that they were the same Benny and Naomi who I'd been told about. They did indeed attend a Messianic Jewish fellowship and would most certainly be willing and able to take me there.

A coincidence? A synchronicity? Luck? I don't know. I try to avoid the "God made it happen" talk, especially when you consider the triviality of this anecdote in comparison to the other things I said above. But it was special and will stay with me as an amazing thing to have happened; a little sign of the underlying magic that's there all the time even when we can't see it.

A few weeks later they took me to a little fellowship of Jesus followers who met on the shores of the Sea of Galilee. The leader was a large man with a big black beard and curly hair; an archetypal image of Peter the fisherman if ever I saw one. Though my faith perspective has changed dramatically since then, this remains for me a wonderful memory of a moment of magic, when all things seemed to be connected, even if on the surface were so disconnected and messy.

* * *

So what now?

Mark, little brother, don't try to understand, don't try to work it all out, don't try to harmonize.

This was always what caused you such stress.

Just let it be and use the things that are helpful to you.

Gauge things by your heart and gut, not your mind.

Your mind is often not your ally.

Deep down you know by natural discernment what is right, good, true, useful. Contradictions don't matter when the things that contradict each other are both helpful.

So, enjoy church services, go for communion, splash holy water as you enter, cross yourself, enjoy the sacred music, and also enjoy your Druid rituals and Wiccan words.

It all has a place within the Great Mosaic.

* * *

Scott Cunningham's book *Wicca: A Guide for the Solitary Practitioner* is certainly having an effect on me. I love what he says about deity. The concept of a loving God and Goddess is a key ingredient of his book. They are seen as natural, close, earthy and warm, and are transcendent as well as immanent. I like the way he describes them. He sees them as a development of the ancient human belief in a mother goddess and father god, mirroring the male/female polarities of much of nature and most living things.

So what was it all about, my experience in the cathedral? It was not really a re-conversion to Christianity. It was, rather, an affirmation of and an enveloping by the dear old Church of England which I still love so deeply. And Christ hugged me tightly there too. He held me and wept alongside me, as if to apologise for all the pain that being part of His church has brought me. Beautiful!

* * *

March, the month of my birthday. It's funny that March comes from Mars (or Ares in Greek) which is the planet of fire, not water like my birth sign. The Piscean planet is Neptune. My birthday is in five hours' time. I'm going to be 42. Boy that sounds so old, yet I feel like a big kid.

It's Lent too, and I haven't thought much about that yet. Lent is symbolic of deserts and denial, of facing one's true, naked, compulsive self. Yet most people use Lent to prove they can give up chocolate, booze or cigarettes. In other words it's an exercise in ego gratification rather than selflessness.

I wonder what Easter will be like this year? Should I celebrate the Eucharist at the retreat I'm leading at The Othona Community in Dorset if I'm asked? I think maybe I should; after all I'm not under the bishop's authority any more.

* * *

Money worries dominate my mind again. This month has been dreadful financially. It's only the first week in March and after tonight that's it for three whole weeks. No more jobs. Of course I won't be idle. There are always piles to do, what with all the various daily pastoral and theological requests sent through the internet, but none of that brings in a penny.

In fact it's worse than that. Right now the next few *months* of my diary are almost totally blank. It's so scary, yet the inner voice is still strong and I do believe I'm doing the right thing. I really do. I am still a priest, but one who is developing a Christian-Pagan way of expressing it.

* * *

I'm driving to Hereford for a knee scan and I popped into my favourite haunt for a bite to eat, All Saints' Cafe. What a marvellous place. It's an active liberal Anglo-Catholic church in a town centre with a high quality restaurant and café. I lit a candle before the beautiful mother goddess statue (the Blessed Virgin Mary).

* * *

A new morning greets me. It's crisp and fresh. We're half-way through Lent and also nearly at the Spring Equinox. I must mark that somehow.

Apart from the amazing cathedral experience, last week was horrible. It brought so many financial worries but this is a new week. And I can see what I did to make last week so unbearable. I allowed the apparent problems to pierce me. I allowed my defences to drop and the fiery darts to make it through the armour.

And what is this armour? Quite simply it's everything I've learned over the years and combined into a spiritual/psycho-logical/therapeutic exercise to jolt me back into the more peaceful and restful place of *now*. It's a powerful thing, the human mind. No wonder the tarot deck depiction for the mind is a whole bunch of razor sharp swords!

I'm reminded of the words I once had engraved onto a key fob, *remember the bigger picture*. Inside, deep down in my heart, I *know how to refocus and heal my own mind*. Deep down, at the very core of my being, I know what is important.

Mark, don't be fooled into thinking that everything has to be neat, clear, unconfused and orderly.

Stop.

Look.

Listen.

Don't try to complete everything within an hour, take time, live the whole experience.

Allow the spirit to flow into what you are doing.

Be doing less and be being.

* * *

I'm sitting next to giant yin-yang. It's my morning walk and I've found a huge grass covered Taoist symbol cut out of the land. It's wonderful because it clearly changes with the seasons, yet always remains yin-yang. It speaks to me of harmony and balance, of peace and joy, of light and dark, of the quest to be here and now in every moment. In a while I will walk through the centre to ritualise my dream of being united to the two sides of my own inner self, my own inner god and goddess.

I'm suddenly beginning to understand how important these morning walks are as a spiritual beginning to each day; a natural, slow in-breath of God/dess energy.

* * *

I've just been sitting with a woman who hears "messages." She wanted advice. It's hard to be put in a place like that. My own "voices" need testing and discerning with care so how am I supposed to advise people on theirs? The most secure place to stand is to see them as being *for you* and yet *from you* at the same time. I'm always very nervous of those so-called prophets who hear messages for *other* individuals. I've seen disastrous results in the past, terrifying ones: "The Lord told me that you must throw away your medication and claim your healing in the name of Jesus."

I can remember a time, back in my Pentecostal past, when a guy from the church showed up at my door saying, "The Lord's told me that you and I need to come out door knocking tonight." He meant evangelising the neighbourhood by visiting random homes, offering those unfortunate enough to answer, a doorstep sermon on being saved by Jesus (who, I'm sure, finds the whole thing very embarrassing).

Well if God had instructed this mad man to call on me he didn't inform him that poor old Mark Townsend had a splitting headache and would rather lick razor blades than go out into the cold, wet and dark winter streets preaching. I told the guy I was ill but he just said, "No you're not. It's a lie from the devil. He's giving you the impression that you are unwell to stop you from doing the work of God. Resist it in the name of Jesus." (I imagine Jesus himself cringing at this point).

But it really hurts I thought. Then, with unsympathetic and over excited fanaticism, he said, "Just believe you have been healed and claim it in the name of Jesus. Then act on your faith. Come on let's get out there."

So the evangelist and his reluctant assistant (who was now dressed in the thickest coat and very odd looking woolly hat) marched out into the freezing night to save souls for the Lord.

After a few hours of doors being slammed in our faces and a throbbing head now ten times as painful, I finally generated enough will power and strength to say "enough is enough. I'm off home to bed."

Needless to say the guy from the church saw this as evidence of my extreme lack of faith, and I imagine he comforted himself (with regard to the lacks of converts) by the thought that it was my weak and pathetically low level of faith that had caused this "victory for the devil" not his own stupid plan.

Looking back, all I can think is "what a couple of pricks."

A few weeks later I saw the same street evangelist bubbling and bouncing with news that his hero (a USA healing preacher who preached a health, wealth and prosperity "gospel") was coming to perform (sorry "preach") at our church. The guy was so excited until (and I had to fight back the tears of laughter) the healing crusade had to be cancelled due to illness! (Jesus: "LMAO")

* * *

Something has just dawned on me. The experience of God I had within the cathedral in Sheffield was truly profound. However I do not in any way (now the experience has had a chance to settle in my mind) wish to cease my journey into Druidry, Paganism and (especially) experience of Goddess/divine feminine.

When I was in that great church I felt an almost tangible sense of the Divine. I melted because it was like returning home to something I'd walked away from. But it was a very male God experience of divine energy. I remember that I had tried to use goddess language within my prayers there, but it just didn't feel right. The encounter I had was one with the church's God and he is usually always depicted as male. The God who became the One True God of the Judeo-Christian tradition has obviously descended from the strong, warrior, MALE, sky God, whereas the earthy, nurturing, maternal and deliciously feminine mother goddess of earth and moon was left out of the developing tradition *or wiped out.*

Obviously she could not be forever held at bay by the church. We can see this within the Orthodox and Catholic traditions that almost deified Mary and made her Theotokos the God-Bearer or "Mother of God."

Modern Christian feminists have (rightly) tried hard to re-feminise this Great Sky God, but for many this is little more than putting a frock on a male rugby player. "God" largely remains a male term in our psyches.

This brings me to a new revelation. My Wiccan reading has begun to show me why there is a duo-theism within ancient (and many modern) spiritual paths. You cannot simply speak of deity (or should I say *symbolise* deity) with one great transgendered God-figure. It's too much. We need to separate our images so we can experience the vastness. Thus Christians only have one half of the picture. It is a true and powerful part of the picture, and last weekend I was reintroduced to it in a beautiful way, but it is only one half nevertheless.

The Goddess, who I'm getting to know now, is a *very new* experience. I've known her implicitly (in Mary and the very feminine portrayal of the prodigal son's dad etc.) but I am now getting to know her personally.

* * *

Oh dear I just did a typical "Mark" thing. It's highly embarrassing to admit but I want this book to be totally honest so I'm going to have to. A couple of weeks ago I decided to paint a big wall picture for my house. My children and I had tried to find something appropriate but just didn't see anything we liked in the shops. So I got myself a large canvas and attempted a painting. It was awful.

So I tried again and achieved a pretty basic painting of Stonehenge. However the people I showed it to were actually quite impressed and one made the big mistake of saying "oh Mark, you could sell those." *DING!* The bell in my mind rang and, sure enough, after a night of art infused dreams, the next day I went out and bought more canvasses, paints and brushes. I'd even returned home having found myself a free gallery to display and sell the pieces from. A shop owner I know was trying to do something different with the upstairs room and had decided on an Art Gallery. She said she was more than happy for me to have an area within the shop for my art, as long as a commission went to the store. So I was off?

A few weeks later, after more money had been spent, the inevitable happened, I crashed. I had ended up doing what I have always said we should avoid at all costs, pursuing goals *for the end result alone*. Arts and crafts, perhaps more than any other hobby or pleasure, ought to be pursued for the satisfaction of the process itself rather than the end product. I had been totally hooked into the product and that alone. In just a few days I'd become obsessed. It all went wrong because I'd noticed that the acrylic paints I'd bought were not very good quality, so I went out and bought some more and they were just as bad, so I got really fed up and said, "to hell with it."

In reality it was a lesson worth learning albeit a little expensive. I spent £50 on a money making project that was not only a non-starter but also went against my own philosophy.

Oh well, it was another wrong turning, but the great thing about wrong turns is that once you recognise that they are wrong turns you can return to the path with more knowledge than when you left it. And when you do so the inner spirit seems to relax, letting you know you've come home.

* * *

I've just been asked to submit 10 spiritual hints for life to a MBS magazine. After the episode with the painting I feel totally unqualified to say anything about the spiritual life. However this is what came to me:

My 10 spiritual hints for life!

1   Be YOU. The real YOU, the YOU who sits silently under the "you" you project to the world.

2   Be unafraid of that YOU.

3   Do not depend on external praise for that YOU, and do not crumble after critics try to punish that YOU.

4   Know that YOU are a spark of God/dess.

5   Know also that YOU, the shining beauty of your deepest self, is often only truly encountered when your outer shell cracks. The ego protects the false-self, whereas the true-self lies underneath all manufactured "goodness" or "holiness." So don't fear the falls, the failures, the bumps and bruises.

6   Know also that falling from the ladder is often a more important lesson than reaching the top. When we place our goals (even spiritual ones) "up there" they are ever out of reach, for the ladder just grows taller. But when we relax, and allow ourselves to fall, we collapse into the truth and beauty of the present moment. In climbing we climb away from ourselves. Falling is the way everything corrects itself.

7   See the inner spark of God/dess as also present within those who judge and hurt you.

8   Remember that just as you find it hard to be the true YOU, so others often lose sight of who they truly are.

9   Each morning, stop for a moment! Breath, listen, be. Be aware and be at one with YOU and your surroundings.

Enjoy being who YOU are, and where you are.

10 And finally always remember the bigger picture. Remind yourself often that nothing is wasted. All is made use of. Everything is recycled. To aid this get a key-ring engraved with the words "The Big Picture!"

* * *

I'm at Avebury's ancient stone circle in South West England. Awesome. It's a 6,000 year old monument that encircles the entire village. How inspiring. I'm sat eating a vegan meal and enjoying a ginger beer. I came all this way to meet someone who doesn't appear to be here, an American Professor and evangelical Christian called Michael Cooper who is researching modern Druidry.

The only land mark I could remember was the gift shop, so we agreed to meet there at 11.30am. I arrived a few minutes late but could not get hold of him by phone because the mobile number he'd given me simply didn't work. It was a dead line.

It's now nearly 1pm. The only thing I can do is finish my lunch, walk the way of the stones, and hope the gods connect us. The trouble is I have no idea who I'm looking for.

* * *

I'm still at Avebury but am now standing high up on the raised circular bank of the outer ring of stones. Directly in front of me lies an enormous moat; the inner stone circle and the village stand at the centre of it. There's a Druid ceremony taking place in front of me.

* * *

I have now walked a little further and had my photo taken under the incredible trees with roots like a sea of rippled water. I will now walk the entire way round and back up to do a little ritual inside two huge stones that I saw on the way round. I love this place.

* * *

As I walked round the whole circle I passed many tourists and pilgrims. I listened out for male American accents and heard quite a few among the number. But I did not approach anyone. It was not until I finished the whole walk and was making my way back through the village to the two great stones that I saw a man standing outside a shop. I walked over and casually began looking in the shop window. Finally I caught his eye and we connected. I said "You're not Michael are you?" He was, and there followed two hours of extraordinary discussion over a pint of one of England's best bitters (well, I had a Coke).

His own theories were astonishing, especially considering his evangelical roots. He had an astrological appreciation of the person of Christ. He believed that early New Testament Christians were polytheistic. He also said that in his opinion Christianity has lost the way and that Pagans have something that could be of huge benefit to Christians.

He was such a breath of fresh air. I heard myself trying to articulate answers to his Christological questions. On this we were different; myself expressing a more progressive stance, but it didn't matter. I really enjoyed hearing a convinced evangelical Christian declare his love and passion for Pagans.

I also felt in safe enough company to share my story of failure and resignation with Michael. He was visibly moved and showed great empathy saying, "My brother I'm sorry, so very sorry. We Christians can often treat our own the worst."

* * *

Because of the visit to Avebury I missed my celebration of the spring equinox with the Cornovii Grove (my Druid community). I also missed the opportunity to celebrate it at Avebury itself (what with time lost in missing Michael). So I decided to do a little ceremony at home, using it as a ritual of planting metaphorical seeds of hope. My spiritual life is still very untidy and unsettled.

* * *

I've been thinking of joining the *Liberal Catholic Church*. If I did I'd be licensed to celebrate Mass again and also remain ordained whilst openly exploring esoteric and more hidden things.

* * *

Amazing. I just went to my local Mind Body Spirit shop, Zenith, and a woman came in who started talking. She obviously knew of me but I did not know her. She talked about a similar journey. She had been badly treated by her vicar. She'd left the church and had started listening to her inner voice which had helped her find a new way.

Then Dawn, the shop keeper, told me about a special place she'd been to the day before. She described it as a gorgeous Welsh waterfall and spring with a Pagan shrine. Everything sounded connected. She showed me a postcard and said, "Mark you just have to go there sometime. I know it will be a special place for you. It will inspire you." I decided that someday I would find the place and pay a visit.

I then went back to my office to check emails and my inbox had something for me, news of my "Druidic initiation." My Druid leader Rob Chapman had just organised a special ceremony to welcome me into the Order as a Bard, and he'd found a very special place (photos were attached). It seemed like a very familiar name, so I looked up the location on the internet and there it was - the very same waterfall in Wales I'd just been shown in the shop.

* * *

I wonder what Easter will mean to me this year? My hunch is that it's going to be quite profound because I'm leading a four-day retreat at the Othona Community, Dorset. The theme is *The Deep Magic of Easter.*

* * *

I just had a very moving phone call from a woman who's asked me to conduct a summer wedding blessing in a forest. Her other half is, like me, an ex-Pentecostal who played electric guitar and sang in the church band. Again, like me, he was one who was on his way to bigger things within the church. The Elders had high hopes for him but then turned against him when his more human side showed its face.

* * *

As my initiation into Druidry approaches I confess to feeling a few twinges of fear. I'm really not sure whether I'll have to be stripped, bound and blindfolded like some Pagan initiations I've read about. My only instructions are, "Bring your robe and some wellies, unless you want to go bare foot."

* * *

I've been doing a little note taking recently and have allowed my mind to wander, carrying me back to past "experiences of magic" (I'm using the term broadly here). This morning I remembered an encounter I had in Africa. I was there on a wonderful exchange trip to visit the various schools, villages and hospitals that my UK home town had connections with. On one occasion my colleague and I drove a rusty old Land Rover out into the wilderness to visit a tiny Massai village (which had been Christianised).

We arrived and were greeted in a typically warm and generous way. An elderly woman amazed me by bowing and saying "Shikamoo" (a greeting which is usually given from the young to the old. It literally means something like "I hold your feet"). I thought it should have been me saying it to her!

We were then taken to their church which was just a tree under which they sat in a circle. The Druid in me thought *how wonderful*. My English priest colleague and I sat down with this community and, as always, we were invited to read "the word of God" and expound it for them. I'm glad that it was my colleague who responded this time, for I had nothing to say. Who was I to tell them anything about God? I'd learned by this time that I knew nothing and that I was learning everything from the people I was meeting.

On our arrival at this little hamlet of a couple of huts and a tree-church, we'd given some pens and pads of paper to the children of the village, and they'd (God only knows how) given us each a bottle of ice cold Coke. The community barely had enough water, yet they'd somehow managed to get hold of two bottles of Coke for their western priest guests. We were treated like kings but we didn't deserve it. We were asked to give the gift of the word of God but had nothing of any substance to say. They had given us far *more* than either of us could ever have given them, yet *they* felt blessed and honoured by *our* visit!

Also my romantic notions of a tree church are misguided in this case, for that community desperately wants a church building where they can meet and keep their books, vestments and other things safe. They showed me how far they'd come in their building project; four posts sticking into the earth. The Elder told me how they were saving up for some second-hand corrugated iron for the roof. I felt so humbled and in awe of these brave, generous and spiritually rich people.

Yes, that visit was one kind of magic, the magic of transformation that comes when you see yourself for who you truly are. First of all you see the "surface you" (for me, it was not a pretty sight). Then you gradually become aware of a "deeper you" (I'm still discovering him).

We drove home knowing how empty and poor we actually were in comparison to these beautiful rich souls (who were literally poor, yet spiritual millionaires). It was a painful alchemical moment for me. One more nudge towards *Truth*.

The second kind of magic that happened a few days later occurred back at our base. I'd been demonstrating some of my sleight of hand magic on a few of the Tanzanians we'd got to know. After a while one of them stood up, smiled a broad smile, and did something I could not believe. He made my head smoke. Yes, he reached out and gently touched the top of my head and made it smoke! I could see the other folk laughing, so I crouched down and looked in the Land Rover's wing mirror. There was a small trail of white smoke leaking out of the top of my head. How? Was it a trick, or was it real MAGIC? What do you think?

* * *

It's mid-March and everything's beginning to make sense. The final connections (or should I say re-connections) are taking place. God, religion, magic, love of nature, mysticism, synchronicity. All this is making sense and fitting into place as I read the beautiful words of Gill Edwards in her book *Wild Love*.

Whereas the "harder" metaphysical spiritual sciences such as *A Course In Miracles*, various forms of modern day Gnosticism and some Eastern non-dualistic traditions scare me by what feels so earth denying, Gill's book makes me want to fall in love with my *forest cathedral* all over again. I was so amazed by what I read in *Wild Love* that I simply had to write to the author. The letter explains what I mean by the comparison between her work and the harder earth denying traditions:

Dear Gill,

I am so excited that I just had to write to you, but I do apologise for interrupting what must be such a busy life.

The reason for my excitement is that I have in my hand a copy of Wild Love. *I was browsing in Waterstones a few weeks ago (after performing a demonstration/lecture for the Leicester Magic Circle) and your book literally jumped out at me and demanded to be picked up. So I did.*

I read Neale Donald Walsh's inspiring foreword (LOVE his books), which reminded me that we often stumble across our own teachers within the most unexpected situations. I had to buy it.

I'm a Priest of the Church of England. But, like many clergy, have had a love/hate relationship with the dear old C of E for many years. It came to a head two years ago when I left full time parish ministry. I'm afraid the present success driven and perfectionist church does not cope well with real, honest, open and flawed individuals like me. I tell the full story of this in my forthcoming book which is called The Path of the Blue Raven (I love ravens. They've become very special to me of late).

I am also a magician (illusionist) and I have used this kind of magic to awaken folk to the deeper magic for many years. Now magic, retreats and writing is what I do for a living.

Gill the reason why your book is such a gift for me is that it is tying together the many loose ends of my experience:

1) I am a Priest and still see the Christ as somehow a symbolic picture of the God-essence of all people, the same as the Jungian

"Self" or the Tibetan "Buddha Nature."

2) I am a magician who also believes in real magic. I am walking the Druid path as well and have found much power from immersing myself in the life-force of forests, streams and open air.

3) I am a writer, who tries to communicate through my books, yet I have not found the necessary key (or maybe now I have?).

4) I adore Eastern philosophy and ideas of the illusory world, but have usually been put off by the harder notions of unreality, illusion and Maya, as if the world we live in is something to be escaped from instead of loved. I want to be more immersed in nature not less. I have also loved reading Western philosophy (from ancient Greek-Gnosticism or modern day equivalents) but it has left me with the same picture, that the physical world is somehow lesser or even (in extreme teachings) evil.

5) I have read much from the world of modern quantum physics, particle science and the spiritual interpretations of it (Bohmian Imax's and Holographic Universes). Yet, again, this has left me with a feeling that our planet is mere illusion and to be ascended or even escaped from. I wrote a chapter in my new book saying that all this talk of holograms and illusion rings huge bells but, as a person with a deep incarnational love of nature, I can't quite take the final step. When I look at my children I do not want to see them as mere illusions, but beautiful beings full of deep magic [hope my waffled words are making sense].

YOUR BOOK is finally giving me the bridge, the link, between all this stuff in my head. It seems that you have been able to come to a place of deep appreciation for the interconnectedness of all things but without having to mentally escape from the planet to do so. I always knew I must have misunderstood what the mystics have been saying. Perhaps I've not been ready for it?

So, Gill, I will read on and look forward to this new adventure. I'm sorry for the long-winded letter but thank you so much for

putting your own thoughts and experiences on paper, so that
confused and messy ex-vicars like me can find hope and wonder.
Yours, magically,
Mark Townsend

* * *

Something strange is happening. The synchronicities are acceler-
ating. There's a deep feeling in my stomach that I am moving into
something new and fresh and magical. Pieces of the messed up
jigsaw are coming together. Loose strands are being woven into
the tapestry. I am discovering what life is, and who I am within
in it.

* * *

I've been thinking about magic and ethics. I'm always aware of
this subject. It's what makes me quite nervous of the magickal
pursuit. What constitutes something being unethical? And when
does the Wiccan 3 fold law of return come into play? Also what
about other people's bad use of magic against me or mine?

My own ethics are pretty clear and firm, even in a non-
magickal scenario. For example those who've made themselves
my enemies, and whom I could seriously hurt (by publicising
how they've attacked me) never taste revenge from me. I do not
fight back with "like for like."

But when I hear stories about people close to me being bullied
at work or at school, or taken for a ride in other ways, I begin to
feel anger welling up inside me. Of course I do not do anything
about it but it makes me wonder what the "magickally powerful"
would do if they were in the same boat.

Do they sometimes just snap and say "enough is enough" and
throw out curses? Can magic turn from good to bad in a flash?
Can good people become bad over night? This is all symbolised

in Star Wars with the story of Anakin Skywalker, Luke's father. He went over to the dark side, not as a quest for power and wealth but due to the pain of living with his own victimhood, losing his parents so violently. The terrifying ordeal of the murder of his parents caused a vengeful streak to fester. There is a fine line between the two magics.

In the end of course love wins in this myth. It is love, the love *of* his son and the love *for* his son, which turns him back to Anakin from his alter-ego Darth Vader.

* * *

God/dess sends his/her little messengers. I was just at a party of a Birmingham church warden. I'd been invited to be *Mr. Magic* for the night and I came across an esoteric couple who'd seen me on TV. They were called Irene and Izzy and they had a glow that radiated warmth. Irene was a healer and, looking at me, said that I seemed tired, anxious and zapped of energy. She said, *"You carry so much worry, heaviness. Be assured, you are protected. You know what I mean don't you? You don't need to worry!"*

She was right about the worry. In fact she was also right that I'd been worrying about being open to uncontrollable forces and energies. Her words brought me some comfort.

* * *

It's nearly Easter and I'm struggling to work out where I stand towards Christianity. I did an online test *Are you a modern Christian Gnostic?* It came out almost 100 per cent positive. But Gnosticism has always sounded so earth denying to me. I'm walking down *The Grange* right now and I can see the fresh spring daffodils and hear the vast array of birds, their voices decorating the soundscape. I love this world. It can't be the product of a false god! But then perhaps I've misunderstood

Gnosticism? If, in essence, Gnosticism points to the underlying oneness, connectedness, the magical link, between all things, and if Christ is that spark of deity which somehow manifests in a very explicit way, but which is essentially our inner nature, then I am a Gnostic.

* * *

I did a funeral today and came across a man I've bumped into many times, but I never realised he was a dowser. In fact I've now discovered he was once one of the leading authorities in the country. He's travelled all over the globe giving talks and lectures to various people, from novices to professors. He shared some truly amazing stories of the things he's witnessed and the people he's helped, some of them very dramatically. What's more, he wants me to visit him so he can pass on some of his knowledge and skills. How exciting, and how fabulous that he's also a Methodist Christian. I asked him how he holds it all together and he just smiled and said "it all compliments."

* * *

I'm so excited. Not only am I going to the Lake District to spend time with the esoteric teacher, Marcus Katz, at his *Far Away Centre*, I've also been invited to meet the author whose book has inspired me so much recently, Gill Edwards. Her book *Wild Love* is the link, the bridge, I've been looking for. It's a bridge that helps fuse together all the various strands of my spiritual journey: The Christian truth of the God of unconditional love, the Pagan love of nature, the Goddess, the idea of there being something *more* than just the physical and especially the goal of a fully authentic life.

I know I couldn't do any of what I am now doing had I not done what I did back in June 2007 and shared my broken story with those in control of my life. All the clergy who tried to stop me were wrong.

My path is now beginning to draw everything together, to close the gaps. It is nothing short of an alchemical journey. Everything I've ever been, and everything I'm discovering, is being slowly melted down and cooked in a great metaphorical cauldron, where it can smoulder and brew and purify to create gold from the lead (mess and muddle).

* * *

The letter I received from Gill Edwards (which included the invitation to meet her) is breath-taking:

[an extract]

A divorced priest - how refreshing! I guess that must have been a difficult journey for you, along with leaving the church. It isn't easy to be that honest with ourselves, in the face of social pressures to be good and perfect. But staying boxed up in anything which does not allow you to be wild and free - whether it is formal religion or a marriage that isn't right - seems crazy once we're out of it. It feels so much better to breathe freely, and be honest about who we are. I had lots of childhood issues around being good and perfect, which were reinforced by becoming a spiritual teacher - but as Wild Love *says, I eventually began to break free from those constraints, and to break the rules around "good behaviour." Authenticity is now a very high priority for me. I think that both religion and relationships are moving into a new era, free from their old boxes and rules and prisons, as we reclaim the divine feminine and become more whole as human beings. And no, nothing is ever wasted. Every experience prepares us for what follows, and helps to expand our consciousness. And Mark, I love ravens too. Many years ago, at one of my workshops where we had been working with power animals and the medicine cards, a raven came to the windowsill of the coffee room. One of the workshop attenders called me to come and see it, as none of them could believe their eyes! One of them had been thinking of giving up smoking, and Raven had come to her in her inner journey. In the break, a real raven had come and taken her cigarette packet from the windowsill! Then it came back and sat there for about ten minutes, staring into the room. Extraordinary. We all felt very blessed - it felt like a divine messenger.*

* * *

I'm busy planning and preparing for *The Deep Magic of Easter* at Othona. I'm going to use Alchemy as a running theme for the retreat. Alchemy is the symbolic process of death, decomposition and re-birth to a purified state. Our metaphorical lead is turned to the purest gold. Life is an alchemical journey and Christ symbolises that journey. As a symbol of an Incarnate God (like we all are) he leads us through the alchemical fires of surrender, breaking apart, disintegration and then resurrection. But also he (and alchemy) can be seen to symbolise the psychological journey of Individuation (Jung), the process of stripping away of the layers of non-self, the many deaths of the voices of the ego, and a gradual re-birth as the *true you*. He says don't fear the breaking, the falls, the little-deaths or the pain. It will (in the end) produce gold.

* * *

I have had another remarkable moment of synchronicity. My plan for the Othona Easter Retreat had progressed to the point where I'd decided to use a tangible *symbol of magic* (perhaps an artefact from a magical legend or enchanted fairy tale) for each session. I had thought of something to use each day, except Good Friday which I was still struggling with. For Maundy Thursday I'd opted for the Magic Carpet from the Arabian Nights (magical travel/symbolic journey) and the Sword of Truth (Judas, Jesus and being true to self); for Holy Saturday the Golden Ball of the Brothers Grimm (losing the symbol of wholeness/Self/and confronting the inner ugliness/shadow/frog prince); and for Easter Sunday the Aladdin's Lamp (accessing the inner genie/wizard/witch). But I was stuck for Good Friday. I needed to find a well-known object from the world of mythology which somehow also symbolises brokenness and destruction. I thought of the phoenix egg, but it's more to do with rising (Sunday) than destruction. The egg is what's found in the ashes of the dead bird, so phoenix ashes would work better than the egg itself, but ash is not a very magical object.

Then came a flash of inspiration. What about the famous philosopher's stone? These days most people seem to be familiar with it from Harry Potter, the artefact of the first book (which ends up in Harry's pocket because he is the only one who desires to find it but not use its power). I thought about it but wondered how I could make it fit the brokenness theme. Then I remembered that alchemy was the ancient process of trying to make gold out of lead. In other words (and in a psychological sense) boil down our false self and end up with the purity of who we actually are. The lead needed to decay, even die, in order to give birth to the gold. On top of this the philosopher's stone, which was the result of such a process, could not only now turn any metal to gold, but also bring eternal life through the elixir of life that was made from it. *Perhaps it's a kind of Eucharistic parallel* I thought. I was getting more and more excited about this idea.

So I would need something tangible, to represent the philosopher's stone, maybe a large coloured crystal. I knew I had a big chunk of amethyst somewhere and thought it might take the role (especially because you have to destroy the outer shell of an amethyst to get to the gorgeous white and purple inner crystal) but the colour didn't really work. I felt the stone ought to be more fire coloured.

I then paid a visit to my favourite shop in town, Zenith, for some inspiration. I found a nice egg that could have done for the phoenix egg, and I also discovered (among the crystals) twenty or thirty orange, pink and honey calcite stones. They were all quite startling and, though the orange ones attracted me more (due to their colour), the largest piece I could find was a honey calcite. In the end I decided to buy it along with a mystically decorated presentation box. I took it home and started looking for themes on the cross, Christ, alchemy and the philosopher's stone. I was amazed by all the connections. Even good old George Herbert had made historical analogies between Christ and the philosopher's stone in his hymns. Also the whole process of alchemy (so I discovered) has indeed been used many times as an analogy for both the life and work of Jesus and the Christian life in general, as well as the Jungian process of individuation. It was all quite amazing.

But then something even more incredible happened. I started to look at gemstone websites and read up on the qualities of the various calcites. I had actually forgotten the name of the stone so I first had to find that by doing a search for orange and honey coloured crystals. Eventually I found a picture of a honey calcite and thought it was very similar to mine. Then I read a little about calcites in general and discovered that the orange calcite is often referred to as *The Philosopher's Stone*. At this point I was not certain whether mine was honey or orange as it was somewhere between the two, so I put it in my pocket and rushed back down to the shop to catch Dawn the owner before she closed. I asked her and she confirmed that mine was honey, so I went back over to have one more look at the orange pieces. As before they were all too small, but then right at the bottom of the pile I came across the biggest of any of the stones, and it was orange. I'd found my philosopher's stone.

* * *

I've just received another astonishing letter from Gill Edwards:

Dear Mark,

I think "long, painful and messy roads" are often the very best, for reasons I talk about in Wild Love. *It is those times of "contrast" which launch huge new dreams and desires - then our only challenge is to get up to speed with what the Universe has now set up for us! Once we know it is a friendly and loving Universe - a primary theme of my recent book,* Life is A Gift - *everything in life becomes easier, even the tough parts. I sent for your* Gospel of Falling Down, *and have already read most of it - so I had just read your dialogues between what I might call your ego and your Deep Self (or just Self). Although your book is very Christian (I guess you would write very differently now), I think you reached very similar conclusions about the value of the dark times, and the wisdom of being honest and authentic about how messy life is - rather than trying to be (or pretending to be) perfect; and about the constant availability of deeper wisdom and unconditional love within. Although you were writing from within the priesthood, it was very clear where you were going. I have now ordered* The Wizard's Gift, *and will take it on holiday next week.*

I woke at 5am today - wide awake - and since I didn't want to read or work, I Googled your name and found myself watching an interview you did for Conscious TV: a really lovely interview. I'm sure we can do something positive together, though I'm not yet sure what. I have passed your name on to Gwyneth Moss, who is organising an EFT Conference in Ilkley, as she was looking for something entertaining and spiritual for the Saturday night - so I suggested she look at your website. I've also wondered this week whether you might offer something similar on my longer workshops, such as my summer retreats - though I have no idea whether this is feasible, given that you live in Hereford, what it would cost etc. Seeing some "real magic" would be a perfect addition to some of my Living Magically workshops - which are designed to awaken the magic within us, and our sense of awe and wonder at life. On my summer retreats, we spend lots of time talking to wise old trees and mountains and lakes, writing poetry, and doing inner journeys, and generally tapping into the right brain. Great fun!

I feel sure there is some way we can help each other, or work together - but I am just playing with ideas right now. And never mind just teaching Kieran some tricks - though he would love that - I would love to know how to do some magic myself! I loved your Enneagram trick on the video. I'm a 5 with a 4 wing, and I guess you are a 4 with a 5 wing. Like you, I find the Enneagram is a really useful tool. I taught it on my summer retreat last year, and people loved it. Seeing where we go under stress, and where our potential lies, is so helpful - and it's great for understanding relationships too.

Must dash. Off to the cinema with a friend.

With love and blessings,

Gill

She was bang on too. I am a 4 with a 5 wing!

* * *

Another of my mentors is Fr. Richard Rohr. He writes the most fantastic spiritual guides from a Catholic perspective. Few Christian authors write or speak with such authenticity as Fr. Richard. One thing he teaches is that with regard to the spiritual life the problem is never *out there*, it's always *you*. Now this is not as harsh as it sounds. He's not encouraging self-blame or self-dislike. Far from it. What he means is that our modern blame culture often (maybe usually) encourages us to point the finger away from ourselves to others who are the cause of our problems. This is completely the wrong way round. With regard to the life of the spirit you are your own problem. You have all the necessary spiritual resources within yourself. Of course the ego hates this kind of teaching. The ego is powerful and constantly demands attention, respect, love and admiration. But we don't *need* to receive that from outside. We first need to give that to ourselves from our own deeper Self, the inner source of unconditional love.

Part of me still demands, "needs" approval, recognition, appreciation. And when I feel it "should" come but does not materialise I react by blaming and demanding and becoming brittle and weak at the knees. What I should do, when this happens, is simply observe myself and then start to remind myself that I have my own inner resources. Genuine love does not depend on this tit for tat, pay back, world of the ego.

* * *

I've been wondering whether my own "need" for unconditional love and acceptance (which can be met by my own inner resources) could also be called a Goddess desire? Could this inner source of unconditional love be symbolised by the nurturing mother goddess? And on this note I've also been considering Mary. While I've always felt that the more excessive Marian doctrines, dogmas and devotions are rather grotesque and so obviously unbiblical (she was human, not divine) I can easily understand the Marian excesses as a natural and beautiful human longing and desire for the divine feminine. My own love/devotion for/to Mary has been on and off over the years. I've been through periods where sacred icons and statues were very important to me and when I used the angelus and rosary daily, but whenever I started to see her as somehow more than human something felt very wrong. However, as a natural symbolic expression of mother goddess, yes.

April

What's gone wrong again? Right now I am at war with myself. My ego is out of control. Like a kicking, screaming child it demands attention. Its voice screams like a spoilt kid: "There you go, see. What's the damn point? Why the hell do you even bother Mark? Why try so hard to make *everyone else* happy when you get kicked in the teeth time and time again? Why don't you just look after yourself and your own needs from now on?"

(To cut a long story short I'd been let down by someone; a person whom I'd done something for as a gift, something that took an enormous amount of time, energy and love).

It's often pure inner madness. My ego voices are sometimes insane. This outburst was all to do with my feeling walked upon and taken for granted again. But the way I reacted was quite unhelpful.

The voice I tend not to be able to hear, especially when I'm in this state, is the deeper, wiser and (dare I say) more motherly voice, what I call the Divine-Me. I can't hear her/him when the ego's complaints are so loud and dominant. During these moments of madness the Divine-Me seems to be asleep.

The fascinating thing about the ego is that it says to those who've hurt us things like this: "You forgot me. Why didn't you remember me? I need you but you clearly don't need me." They are voices of dependency, yet on the other hand they can also be hostile, defensive and rejecting, angrily claiming total independence: "See if I care. I don't need you."

However the Divine-Me just keeps loving. The Divine-Me sees from the other perspective. The ego can only see from its own limited view point. The ego tries to self-protect and keep you safe by how it acts, but (ironically) creates inner warfare on a huge scale and ends up attacking you and making you feel anything but safe and secure. The true self, who does not try to protect the smaller self but lets go and trusts in the bigger picture is actually, in the long run, your true friend. It is your true you.

Mark, you only have to love.

You don't have to hate your ego.

You don't have to argue or tell it to shut up, or grow up.

Neither do you have to respond to its demands.

Simply observe it.

Allow it the freedom to express itself, then love and forgive it, but know also that it is not in fact the real you. It is the manufactured you!

Mark, you can easily test whether these voices are the real you or not.

If they end up making you feel smaller than yourself, deflated, tense, grasping, defensive, childish and needy then they are of the ego.

Simply acknowledge them and let them go.

When you do so you'll gradually become more accustomed to the deeper truth of who you are.

The other night my little-me voice was so strong that I totally identified with him and got locked in ego-mode. I couldn't break free. And now no amount of self-analysis will help. I can't sleep because I'm over analysing and all that energy comes from the ego. Whereas when I get in touch with the deeper self I begin to relax. The deeper self *does not need* to know reasons. The deeper self is simply at peace with everything as it is. The deeper self is unlimited love.

Mark, go to bed, sleep now.

You do not need answers.

You do not need to know why this or that happened.

You are as you are.

And as you are is loved by God/dess which is also the voice of the deep Self.

Rest now.

Sleep in peace.

* * *

I am sitting at my altar. My God/dess candles lighten the space and I pray for a sword of truth to cut away anything inauthentic within me, the layers of manufactured self, the hats I wear, the masks I hide behind. The morning office for April from Tess Ward's book *The Celtic Wheel of the Year* expresses it beautifully:

> Praise to you Honest Spirit, who requires that we meet you in truth and weeps over us when we do not see the depths of our deceit. Call to my deep, O deep natural God that I might come as I am and allow you to reveal my masks.
> *(Tess Ward, The Celtic Wheel of the Year, O-Books. 2007 p. 80).*

I sit here now, a living example of the results of an ego turned inward. I am an image of what Fr. Richard Rohr alludes to when he says that the true enemy of peace (in terms of the spiritual life) is not "out there" but "right here." The problem is not "him" or "her" but you.

Last night in bed I allowed my imagination to drag me out of the present moment and back into the painful memories of the past, and whenever this happens I get dislodged from reality and plunged into unreality. This is where the sword needs to come and pierce all illusions. I cannot change the external world. The only option is how I see it, how I respond to it.

Swords cut and cause pain, but the wound once healed is then a *truer me, a more real you.* As I cut away these layers by simply observing, acknowledging, forgiving and letting go, the me under all the baggage begins to be seen more brightly and more powerfully.

* * *

Gill Edward's book is still tying so much together for me. Her analysis is amazing and ties in with so much of what I tried to say in my book *The Path of the Blue Raven*.

The Sky-God image was adapted by the Judeo-Christian religions and the Earth Mother was gradually denigrated and finally eliminated from mainstream religion, so all monotheistic faiths ended up out of balance with overarching male deities of power and no real concept of the divine feminine. The Sky God religions were much more "separatist and sacrificial" than the Earth Mother in their notion of deity. The Sky-God religions morphed into an image of a divine God of light who demands atonement.

As far as Christianity went God (in Jesus Christ) in a remarkable twist however, took up the Sky-God image, becoming the Sun God himself, and also made use of the sacrificial system but destroyed it from within (an inside job) saying "no more, God does not do sacrifice."

The trouble is that the male church couldn't cope with femininity so not only did the early church purge all traces of the goddess from the faith, it also turned Jesus' anti-sacrificial demonstration into a supremely sacrificial rite which ended up as The Mass thus perpetuating the split spirituality, the state of separation between heaven and earth.

* * *

I've just watched a great TV programme called *Only the Small Things*. It's a series about a church choir and it's so realistic. Some of the characters have come straight out of a typical parochial church council meeting. It's all about the usual scandals and affairs you get in other sit-coms and plays, but this one's really special. The plot is to do with a choir that thinks it's better than it is and the choir master's desire to manipulate it into a more professional set up, which requires some necessary pruning. However his ex-wife hates the bullying, bullshit and pretense, and comes up with the idea of creating a church music group (rock band really).

The scary thing was that I recognised some of the characters of the many different church sub groups and committees I've been part of. I laughed at the play, but underneath I was angry too. I've seen people treated so horribly in churches. Yet much of my anger was directed at me because I was not strong enough to stand up for all the people who were being bullied. I admit that I was scared and I allowed myself to be intimidated by them.

Quick, pinch yourself Mark. There, see, you're free now.

* * *

It's a beautiful spring morning. The sights and sounds of *The Grange* are amazing today. All around me is an orchestra of sound, from the gentle coo coo of the dove, to the occasional hammering of the woodpecker. Signs of new life are everywhere. Primroses decorate the ground and tiny green leaves begin to revive some of the trees that have been sleeping through winter. All of it is a display of the continually shaping, shifting, changing faces of Mother Nature.

I need this to re-kindle my connection to nature because I've felt a little disconnected again recently. The inner turmoil and confusion with regard to "where I stand spiritually" has robbed me of some of the security and peace I used to experience.

It's a peaceful moment now though. The unhurried enjoyment of the blissful present is my natural state. It is everyone's natural state, once we've cut away the self-manufactured illusions that separate and judge and attack and defend and cover up the deeper me (you).

Gill Edwards has become my new teacher. She has reconnected me to a deep and loving aspect of deity that had become muddled and lost within all my polytheistic confusion.

* * *

We've just arrived in heaven, a place on the South coast called *The Othona Community* (based in Dorset). It was a lovely four and a half hour drive with my wonderful daughter who's so wise. She and I had such a fabulous, open discussion on the way. I'm so proud of her. I hope my son's ok back at home. I just wish he was with us too.

I'm sitting in my room where I can look out at the beautiful garden and sea beyond, a vast expanse of clear blue water on a gorgeous coastline. I'm very happy to be here and am wondering with anticipation what the Great Spirit has in store for us. I've brought my priest's garments in case I'm asked to say Mass on Easter Day. I feel like I'm a vicar again. Thank you my God/dess.

* * *

It's Good Friday. Last night's Maundy Thursday session went very well. We used the image of the magic carpet and I showed them a "real" one to introduce the theme of the magic of the imagination. I also talked about value and what made Jesus valuable. To some it was merely the bag of silver coins. To others his value was as a teacher and so on.

It was a good session. I wanted to begin the whole four days with the question, *What makes a person valuable?*

Today's Good Friday session was also very productive. I used the story of the broken vase from Mary Poppins, which is all about a stressed out father re-gaining his childlike ability to play after breaking a priceless vase and finding the little stars he'd hidden inside it when he was a boy. We also discussed the magical symbol of the philosopher's stone. There followed a remarkable discussion on the benefit of brokenness and using our weaknesses for good, with contributions from both adults and children. We even got into atonement theory.

* * *

I've just wandered down to the beach with my daughter. We're sitting by the edge of the ocean together. It's so beautiful; two water sign dreamers gazing into the vast expanse, a great a symbol of the deep unconscious, each thinking our own thoughts and refusing to be put into a box. She is so like me, only a lot stronger.

* * *

Jorvik and Dagmara, two Polish volunteer workers at Othona, gave me the privilege of performing a traditional Polish custom for them. On Holy Saturday hard boiled eggs, salt and bread are brought into churches to be blessed symbolically to be used on Easter morning. Dressed in my priest's robes, these are the words I put together for them:

Jen Dobre.

Heavenly Father, we give thanks that we are all one family, that the Christ, the spark of deity in all people, unites us whatever our background, tradition, culture or experience. We are all gemstones within the Great Mosaic of God. And, to wonderfully remind us of this oneness, we will now use this beautiful Polish tradition.

We also give thanks for Jorvik and Dagmara, for their ministry here and their gifts.

In Poland every Holy Saturday eggs, bread and salt are brought in baskets to the parish church. This happens all day long and every member of the community has a role to play.

Then the priest says words of blessing reminding the people of the significance of each offering.

Heavenly Father,

Bless these eggs as a sign of new life – the new life we celebrate tomorrow as we share them at breakfast.

Bless this bread as the sign of Christ – our heavenly nourishment and sign of the God who lives within all.

And bless this salt as the sign of humanity – salt of the earth – may we all bring taste, healing, energy and life to our own communities.

In the name of the Father, Son and Holy Spirit.

Then I said the final part of the blessing in Polish.

* * *

It's the morning of my initiation into a new stage of my spiritual adventure. I'm spending some time at *The Grange* where I'm enveloped in sound again. All around, my feathered friends sing and make music. And just to my left is, surprisingly, the full moon. It's nearly 8am and yet the moon goddess still shines meeting the sun-god in harmony of purpose. It's Easter Monday.

Yesterday I celebrated Easter Day as a priest at Othona. I put on the chasuble and used my own liturgy. It felt good. I was there, in the midst of a group of people, some of whom were committed Christians, others were hurt ex-churchians, others were from different faiths and still others were of no faith. But it felt right. I stood there and represented all of us, the mish mash of beliefs and confusions. The Mass was quite wonderful but I did not feel I was celebrating a churchian ritual. It felt like the special ceremony to remember a friend of humanity who was not the founder of a new religion but the corrector of a religious mindset.

I still have far to go in my quest to bridge all the gaps and fully understand my place within this Christian-Paganism but I now have hope that all will one day be harmonised. Today I will become a ritually initiated Bard within the Druid tradition. I will take with me my friend Jesus and all my other friends who've helped me reach this far, among them Neale Donald Walsh,

Thich Nath Than, Ekhart Tolle and so on.

* * *

My initiation

I'm here. I'm sat on a huge mossy rock, half way up a Welsh mountainside. It's like heaven. The grass on the ground is decorated by tiny daisies and primroses. There's a stream bringing fresh spring water trickling past my feet and down to the valley below. Rob (the Chief) has left me here while the rest of the group climb on up and prepare the place for me.

There's so much clutter in my head this morning. Someone from my past rang my mobile this morning (a missed call) triggering all sorts of unwanted thoughts. But now, here, alone, yet in the company of the spirits of place, my head begins to settle. My mind gently wanders back in time to another initiation I once went through, when I was sitting on a different, yet similar, rock in a hot New Mexican desert. Here, however, I feel the sweet texture of Mother Earth beneath me and am enveloped by the green and lush countryside amid the soothing sounds of small birds and running water.

Am I ready to take this next step? Yes.

I'm ready Great Spirit. What do you want of me.

Little brother let go.

Let go of everything and trust.

Trust like never before.

Let yourself be taken by the hand and brought through a new doorway into a bright and rich magical realm.

Leave behind all the nightmares of the past. Leave behind the Mark of ego who still seeks to control and make reality happen. Instead let go and be carried. Open yourself to the voice within, to the new path, to all that is.

* * *

The initiation was spellbinding. And the great Vegas based magician Jeff McBride sent a message to me for the occasion:

> *Your initiation points the way to the new spiritual road ahead of you, a road that transcends all religions. It is said that religion is for people who are afraid of hell and spirituality is for people who have been there and back. Your work as a bard is to create a sonic map; a road crafted by your words that can lead our friends from hell, back to heaven that is there on earth.*

I told my friend and fellow Anglican priest, Caroline, all about it. I also explained how Dawn (from the MBS shop) and Rob (who do not know each other) both showed me a photo of the place on the same day. Caroline responded by forwarding me something she'd sent me a few years before; some liturgical words with a picture. Amazingly (and unknown to Caroline) it was yet another photo of the same waterfall, and the words that went with it were incredible:

An adaptation of Zechariah 14:8-10

In both summer and winter, life giving streams will flow from Jerusalem, half of them to the Dead Sea in the east, and half to the Mediterranean Sea in the west. Then only One Source of Life, Midwife God, whose deliverance is in healing and justice in peace and in love, will be known.
(A short time of silence)

In the womb of beginnings
Mothering God
formed dawn and dusk
sun and starlight,
whispered breath of life into creatures and companions

*and willed our birth
to be a beginning of fullness of life.*

*Mothering God who gathers us from east and west, north and south,
that we might sing together your praise
and know your brightness in our hearts,
Send us out to be your life giving streams in the dance of your
creation.*

*Mothering God, Source of Life, bless our journey,
remind us of the wells of tradition to draw from,
the spring of the living water of Christ
and the ceaseless flow of the Holy Spirit.*

Be with us as we journey.
Be with us as we journey.

**The Peace of the God our Mother, the Source of life be with us,
Shalom.**

* * *

I'm at the crematorium in Hereford officiating at a funeral for a
lovely Catholic family. I'm reading from a book about St. Francis
because, though a Catholic family, they are (as they described)
"Christians outside of the church," and I've always seen Francis
as a Saint who saw the Divine outside of churches rather than
within them. It sometimes occurs to me just what a bridge this
saint of poverty was between the Christian and Pagan worlds. He
called the sun his brother, the moon his sister, the earth his
mother and saw all creatures as his family.

During the funeral I said "if a church had 100 worshippers,
you'd find there were 100 different religions." The man whose
funeral it was had not fallen out with the church exactly but had

certainly moved beyond its narrowness. After service the family all said "yes Mark, good point." One of them, the son, said "gosh you're so right Mark. My wife and I are both Catholics and we are poles apart on almost everything as far as religion goes." I replied, "I'm sure that is how it is for many and it's quite normal and healthy. Faith is, after all, such a personal thing. It's like any other human taste or preference."

I remember one time at theological college when, asked to define the gospel, I suggested there were as many gospels present as there were people in the room. Of course these different gospels are all, in the end, refracted colours from the same single divine source. I think this is another reason why modern eclectic Paganism works so well. It does not see such difference and diversity as a threat or odd; in fact it tends to celebrate it.

* * *

I'm sitting in a beautiful riverside hotel on the banks of the Thames in the little village of Sonning. I just popped into one Inn and the drinks were so overpriced I've had to come to another. But here I have to wait until 12.25 when I go and visit Uri Geller. I phoned him from my mobile a few moments ago and he said to call by at 12.30. It seems odd really, a man I first heard of when I was collecting magazines called *The Unexplained* back in my childhood. He's someone who's had an enormous influence as a mystic and man of mystery. In many ways Uri is more of a mentor to me than even some of the big magicians I admire, because this man clearly believes that magic puts people in touch with magick.

I decided to briefly visit Sonning parish church. The smell of Easter lilies was breath-taking when I entered this exquisite building. I think it's the first time I've ever been consciously filmed on CCTV when entering a place of worship!

*God, Great Spirit, Source of all and known by many names, thank
you. Thank you for holding me as I've walked this often lonely road.
You're here now. I know you are. I can sense you.*

I wonder what Uri's going to be like. Will he see me as just
another wannabe or will he detect the deeper me beneath the
surface?

* * *

Oh my God! I just spent over an hour with Uri Geller. What a
lovely man. He came into the room, rushed over and embraced
me, sat me down and gave me a copy of his new book (which he
had ready and prepared). He then signed it and decided to draw
me an original picture on the first page. I gulped as a saw him
draw a symbolic bird that looked remarkably like a raven!

We talked and he gave me some good advice. We also chatted
about synchronicity and I noticed a tiny wooden kaleidoscope on
his table. I found that amazing because a kaleidoscope is one of
the five gifts that are given to my character Sam in my book *The
Wizard's Gift*. And I'd brought that very book as a small gift for
Uri. Apparently someone had left the kaleidoscope there, and he
didn't know what it was. When I explained he became like a little
boy on Christmas Eve. I then told him about the raven picture,
the raven book of mine and the fact that I was about to go and
visit a raven sanctuary that very afternoon. He told me that only
yesterday he'd moved his raven statue from right where we sat to
his London residence.

After about an hour his personal assistant came in and asked
whether he was ready to be interviewed. Uri explained that every
week he spoke on a USA radio show. He invited me to go on air
with him and told me that, if I do, I'll get to speak to about 8
million American listeners. His PA set up the studio and Uri was
on. He then said, "Hello friends, you know today I have an
amazing young man with me who I'd like to introduce you to.

He's a priest who's also a *sorcerer!*" I did a little impromptu mind reading and got everything bang on. Uri sat opposite me smiling with delight and giving me the thumbs up as I left the American interviewer spellbound (not bad for a totally unprepared interview).

* * *

After leaving Uri's house I went on to visit a place I first heard about on a TV programme called *Springwatch, a* raven sanctuary for injured corvids called Raven Haven. What a treat to spend some time with my soul birds. I had to stay in the area outside the huge fenced off areas where the birds lived for about two hours, so they could get used to my presence. Then I was allowed inside to meet the birds face to face. They were huge, elegant and very cheeky. One tricky raven flew up and landed on my shoulder. Then he pinched my prized Magic Circle lapel badge flying off with it. I never got it back.

* * *

I'm now on a train to London but still feel rather over-awed by all that happened yesterday. Uri was fantastic and the ravens were amazing. Today I go to the ITN studios, London (hopefully to perform some magic for the producers). Then I'm off to visit a wedding couple. I may also try to visit two of the oldest occult booksellers while down here.

The ITN meeting went well. They might do a documentary on me in the style of the series called *The Tribe*. But this would be about a vicar who's a magician and into Paganism. I'll leave it up to them and the will of the universe. After that I met Toby and Linda to discuss their wedding and they were so special. We really clicked and I feel deeply honoured to be doing their forest service. Toby's story reminded me of how, when I was a

Pentecostal, two of my friends were kicked out of the church for having an affair. They were "handed over to Satan!" What crap! And what made it worse was that, back then, I had been willing to go along with the church's decision. Poor Toby had a similar experience when he was a young person at the Vineyard church.

* * *

I'm walking down *The Grange*. It's late April and it's so beautiful. The changing colours are exquisite, fresh green leaves sprouting and flowering on the branches. And other colours too, oranges, purples, pinks and more. And birds, their glorious sounds fill the air.

* * *

I couldn't get to a Beltane celebration this weekend but today I am at the very beautiful All Saints Anglo-Catholic church in Hereford. I love it here. Smoke and bells, flowers and statues, a very Christian-Pagan style of worship.

David, the young priest, blew my mind with his sermon. He spoke of the contrast between ideas of the resurrection of the body as opposed to the immortality of the soul and suggested the latter (a Pagan idea) has been more prevalent. It was the first sermon I'd asked for a copy of for years. It reminds me of an ongoing debate between me and a close friend who's also a priest. In fact our debate began back when we were together at Theological College. He still holds that the only true Christian belief about death is resurrection of the body and that there's no room whatsoever for the belief in the immortality (or transmigration) of the soul.

In stark contrast to the wise and compassionate tone of the sermon were the prayers. A lay server stood up to read them and they were heavy and judgemental in tone, "Lord purge the church of all corruption and immorality" and so on. He came out with lots of "may we live in the light and let the light shine." I found them totally dualistic and oppressive prayers.

I've just received communion and now sit looking at the altar, the crucifix and six candles and, above, the gorgeous blue stained glass. The most dominant and obvious part of the window is the huge and beautiful mother and child image. She stands on the crescent moon and has a crown of stars over her head; the Mother Goddess I think.

* * *

One of the amazing books I'm reading at the moment contains some of the most beautiful descriptions of divine encounters I've ever read. It's an academic book called *Pagans and Christians* by Gus DiZerega, a third degree Gardenarian Wiccan. His description of meeting the Goddess is breath taking. He describes an experience of suddenly feeling himself being immersed in a sea of perfect and limitless divine love. "There is no greater nor more perfect love than that from the Ultimate," says DiZerega, "The experience [of divine love] encompasses complete understanding and unconditional acceptance, neither of which are purely human capacities." And, "Because divine love is unconditional, each being would be treasured and cherished, regardless of whether that love was returned."

Gus DiZerega, *Pagans & Christans, The Personal Spiritual Experience* (Woodbury MN: Llewellyn Worldwide, 2001) p.93

* * *

Today's been one of the nicest days I've had in a long time, gardening with my daughter. And I was just thinking how perfect it all was, and how magical something like digging can be, when up above us two ravens flew straight over. I find it more and more amazing how these rare birds (who should not even be in this geographical area) choose to fly right over my house. Perfect.

* * *

I'm off to Westfield School today. How lovely to be going back there. It is a school for children with special needs which I used to visit as a vicar. Now I do assemblies as a magician. Their smiling faces brighten many a gloomy day.

* * *

A new funeral has just come in. The poor deceased man's will was to be buried in his family grave at a particular Herefordshire Village churchyard but, because of a combination of him moving away and church regulations, he can't be. The family is upset by the situation and the unbending rules, so they have come to me.

* * *

I'm now sitting amongst the delegates of the Litchfield Diocesan Convention. They invited me to lead a Soulful Magic session and being with them has been a real joy. I've met some old friends and have also made new ones. This morning at breakfast I shared my story, and the warmth was tangible. One old vicar said to me "you'll be ok Mark; He won't let you go. You'll be back." I performed for them last night and it was amazing. Their reactions were wonderful. Many of them said how enlightening it had been, and a few were even magicians themselves, so I gave them a little impromptu teaching session after the performance.

I'm now sat in a huge conference room and a leader is getting us to sing some chants (the Agnus Dei and Gloria). It's sweet and soothing being here.

One of my favourite theologians, Dr. Paula Gooder, is going to lecture. I know Paula from my college days, where she taught Old Testament. She was inspirational on Jewish Merkavah Mysticsim which she taught with passion. Merkavah was the precursor to Kabbalah.

Her lecture was stunning. She touched on my old chestnut, resurrection and the immortality of the soul. The Greeks, she said, believed in the transmigration of the soul. The body dies and the soul leaves the body. So she asked us what we believe, and then went on to say that most modern New Testament scholars would say that the New Testament is totally resurrection based (i.e. the body will die and you will remain in the ground until you rise). She told stories about pastoral encounters with people she's spoken to who were gutted when they heard this stuff, and asked things like "so where's mum now?' Paula's experience is that everyday people generally do not understand death the way the New Testament does. They actually believe in the immortality and transmigration of the soul. Paula suggests that we need to discuss these things more openly.

* * *

I've just heard back from the couple I met in London whose marriage I'm going to bless within a forest:

Hi Mark,
We had a major disaster today which was rescued by a raven. Lin's going to tell you about it. It was really weird. I was song writing yesterday. When I write I tend to just play and naturally find a tune that lifts me, and then I let out whatever I see in my mind or feel wants to come out. Well yesterday I was singing about a raven showing us the way. I just saw it in my mind and I didn't tell Lin anything about it. You know there is definitely something going on within me. Anyway here's Lin.
Toby

Hi Mark,

Now are you ready for something amazing?

Toby and I went to Ashridge today to have a double check about parking for the wedding. We met the lady in charge and started to talk about areas we could use for cars, as they get so busy. We took a walk over to the meadow and looked at the site, and there were caravans in the field. I couldn't believe what I was seeing and tentatively asked if they would be there on the day and was told "yes it's the caravan and camping club, and in August there will be more" (how come we were not made aware before!).

I hated it. It looked like a campsite. All of a sudden the picture of my beautiful "isle" turned into an image of children playing football, people on blankets, and the whole area covered in vans. It wasn't what I had in mind. Toby's initial response was "we have no time to change it" and I spent the next ten minutes fighting back tears.

We talked about it and both felt the same. I cannot describe to you the gut wrenching panic and disappointment I felt. Hot tears of fury, frustration, and this deep pain of "oh no it's this late in the day and it's all going wrong again." We have had so many setbacks and finally thought we'd sorted things out but now this. A difficult discussion ensued. I pulled myself together in the name of serendipity, and we set off to explore some more of the area. Toby felt we should drive out and look around the outskirts.

We looked around, nearly had a row, and then found ourselves at again another stalemate. He wanted to drive out further and I wanted to stay, so we agreed to separate and see what we could find and then meet up and compare. I stomped off, trying to believe there must be a reason for it and trying to remain positive. I walked further and further, knowing I was deviating from the path near the car parks and not caring. I can't tell you why I went the way I did but just carried on as the further I went the calmer I felt (I was so upset).

I walked for ages and began to feel hungry and tired. I also began to think that Toby was right. Within 7,000 acres of woodland how on earth would we find a clearing? Maybe it was better to drive out to the edges of the estate, but then that would have been like getting married in an old field on the edge of the road. I stopped, put my head in my hands and said out loud, "oh god help us." When I removed my hands, I naturally turned my face upwards and opened my eyes – and there it was, a raven flying across the sky. It uplifted me. I thought of you and I thought maybe it was showing me something. Maybe if I just go on a little further. It flew off, and then returned. I carried on and took another path. My heart soared as it suddenly got very quiet. I thought again that maybe this was meant to be as the meadow that we originally planned for was noisy and, on later reflection, could not have been the right spot.

I began to hear the sounds of the leaves rustling in the trees, which I love as it sounds like waves. The passing trees started turning into silver birches with their little leaves and tall branches, and I found myself enveloped by an area within a clearing. I thought "Wow - is this it? Is it possible?" I walked on and found another possible site, and there they were - two sets of two trees that stood out, but one of them had a third behind it and they looked majestic. These two trees, with another right between them set back were entrancing. I looked around and it was just how I imagined it to be, better than the meadow and actually within the forest. I couldn't wait to find Toby and started wondering whether they would allow it to be held there, and how long we have to wait to find out.

I made my way back but not before I looked up and said "thank you." Then I went back to the car to find Toby sitting there and looking defeated. I said "come with me, the raven showed me the way." He said, "Oh my God, I was singing about a raven flying in the sky and 'showing us the way' only yesterday." I said, "Well, there you go then. It's meant to be." Toby found the connection between the raven and his song quite a coincidence but the best moment of all came as we made our way back up to the spot I found. Toby was marveling about how I saw a raven, and he was singing *about a raven, and I could tell he was missing something. I said, "Toby you know the other amazing thing don't you?" He said, "No." I said, "Well what would you say if I told you Mark's new book is called 'The Path of the Blue Raven?'" "You're joking," he said and then added, "Now I'm really freaked out."*

He went pale and was totally overwhelmed. I was too, but I also am used to these kinds of experiences, not to the point they don't surprise and delight me but I know that this happens, so watching him was priceless. We went and looked, and he fell in love with the site. We both had a hug, and then I looked at him and said, "so is this it, have we rescued it, do you want to do it here?" He said, "yes, it's the place, either one of those two sets of two trees." ("the cypress and the oak grow not in each other's shadow." Kahlil Gibran).

We had another hug as we agreed that it was the right place, and then Toby said "Look!" The raven then flew over the site, right across the skyline, almost as if to say "glad you like it, take care then." TRULY MAGICAL!

We then dragged the lady back there and had the scary chat about whether we'll be allowed. She needs to talk to a warden and check no wild flowers need protecting etc. so fingers crossed.

Take Care Mark,

Linda x

* * *

I've been involved in a thread on Gus DiZerega's blog on Beliefnet called *A Pagan's Blog*. He was discussing the excellent book by River and Joyce Higginbotham called *Christopaganism: An Inclusive Path*. I guess he wanted to check me out and tried to clarify whether I saw my own Christianity as "a particular way of honouring and loving one another and the sacred in all things, which includes sacred immanence as well as sacred transcendence." I replied and agreed adding this:

I also agree that this is the core of truth in every spiritual way of life and that it is certainly not "the definition of Christianity that has characterised its advocates historically or currently."

The whole problem (in my opinion) is that Christianity began with a gust of fresh air, a wave of new life, a vision which had the impact of "cutting out the religious middle man" and bringing people back to the older (and more Pagan) notion that deity can be experienced by all, personally, and without the need of temples, priesthoods or any form of mediator.

This wonderfully rebellious prophet simply wanted to re-awaken the divine within all those he came across. He therefore transformed the lives of the powerless and those who'd been spat out by the institution, and consequently pissed off those who ran the institution (even though the gift of a renewed vision was for them too). The consequence for him was of course death!

Jesus did not intend to create Christianity. He simply wanted to repair his own tradition from within. But his message still speaks to people outside of his original tradition and situation, for it encourages us to see the divine in ourselves and in one another and (I believe) in all things. Thus Jesus' real message is truly universal and is also (ironically) nothing to do with converting to this or that denomination or religion, but simply knowing that there is no need to ever feel separate from the divine, and that essentially all are capable of goodness.

* * *

I'm back at *The Grange* and, while there, have been greeted by the ravens again!

May

Its Beltane time, the Pagan start to summer and the festival of nature's greening and re-birth, of growth and fertility. I'm at *The Grange* and the green is vivid today. It's so bright that it's very near luminous. My chlorophyll green cathedral is rich with shimmering energy, life force. A creation centred scientist once said how biologically close a relative the life force of plants (chlorophyll) is to the life force of mammals (blood).

* * *

I'm now sitting near the river in Putney, London, spending a little time on my Druid course before I have to prepare myself for a wedding (though as entertainer rather than celebrant today). I'm a little nervous as this is a biggy; three hours of close up sleight of hand and then a cabaret magic spot.

* * *

Well, after the very long day of travel the wedding magic went very well indeed. They turned out to be a lovely couple from Vietnam. It was such a pleasure to perform to a Vietnamese audience (with lots of Scandinavians present too). I used to sponsor a little Vietnamese girl called Thu. I wonder how she's doing now. I stopped sponsoring her just before I left the church. My old parish took over the sponsorship. I hope they still keep in touch with her and the family.

I ended the show with my favourite snowflake effect, a lovely symbolic blessing for the special day. One of the young men came up to me and asked if I knew Qi Gong. He'd seen me bend some metal cutlery (Uri Geller style) and wondered what "powers" I had been developing. Another guy gave me a £20 tip; something that had never happened within that context before. How lovely.

It's also the 4th May and I've spoken to my amazing son Jamie, on the phone. It's his twelfth birthday. It's so hard being away from my kids, especially at special celebratory times like birthdays, but I have to take every booking possible at the moment.

* * *

I'm in Canterbury now, performing at a school where an old friend of mine from Hereford Diocese works as a Chaplain. Gosh I can see our Mother church in the distance, Canterbury Cathedral. I'll have to pay a visit while I'm here.

* * *

I'm inside the cathedral. I tried to pop to see the Dean (who I also know from his Hereford days) but no luck; *busy*.

This is a stunning place indeed. So much history lies right under my feet, not least Beckett's gruesome murder. I've just walked up to the site of his medieval shrine, now simply marked with an eternal flame. A certain King Henry (V) had him killed and then another King Henry (VIII) came along and ransacked his shrine some 400 years later. It was moving to walk past the spot and look at the high altar and (replica of) Augustine's chair, imagining the fate of this most brave and remarkable Englishman. He was one of those who stood up against what was clearly wrong, even when it was personified by his own best friend Henry V. He was truly a converted man of God.

* * *

I've just met with my good old friend from theological college, a fellow Church of England priest. What a great guy and great vicar. In fact what a total mad-man, which is why I love him. I don't know whether he's a non-realist or a pantheist now. He always makes me think, which is great.

* * *

Wow I've just been approached by the acquisitions editor of the oldest and biggest Pagan book publisher in the world, Llewellyn. She's asked me about submitting an idea for a new book. After a little consideration I think I want to write a book on Jesus for Pagans or even on Jesus but through *Pagan* eyes. Yes, how's that for a title, *Jesus through Pagan Eyes*. Not only will I be able to talk through some of my own issues and explorations, I may also be able to interview Pagans of various paths about their views on Jesus.

It could be a book to:

1   Highlight the spiritual value of Jesus from outside the church's perspectives.
2   Be a source of material for ex-Christian-Pagans who still want some kind of relationship with him.
3   A source of joy and spiritual refreshment for those still inside the church but who would like a new picture of their master.

* * *

I've now heard back from the USA publisher. They're very interested in my potential book proposal. How exciting!

I've been reading some blogs on Christo-Paganism. There seems to be some ambivalence toward it, even distrust. This is a shame because Neo-paganism is generally so eclectic and non-dogmatic, and actually blends many paths. I've come across a huge amount of Dru-Witches for example, and even a few Jew-

Witches. And there are thousands of Pagans who happily use god and goddess images from Hinduism or immerse themselves in the Hebrew Kabbalah. Surely there are some Christian elements than can be of value to Pagans and vice versa.

* * *

It's the Cornovii Grove (my local Druid group) Beltane ceremony tomorrow, hurrah. I'm taking my 12 year old son with me. He's getting very keen on Paganism. The adventure continues.

* * *

Today I watched that famous clip of the plastic bag dancing in the wind from the film *American Beauty*. It's perhaps one of the most evocative scenes ever to hit the screen. the narrator describes the beauty of the moment, as the bag dances in front of him begging him to play and suggesting that there's a kind of divine benevolence behind everything, and thus no reason to fear. I so relate to that. These last few days have seen old fears thrown up to tempt my mind again. The "what ifs" that stop you doing what your gut tells you you should do.

Well, now I'm sat on a hill, looking out over the countryside and everything does seem safe, held, and at peace within the benevolent life force of all things.

* * *

Last night I watched a film with my kids, *Yes Man* starring Jim Carrey. It's a comedy but is yet another movie that moved me deeply. It rang loud bells of recognition within me. When you say "yes" to what is, yes to life, rather than resisting it and allowing your inner conversation to bring in reasons why to say "no," the universe begins to work in your favour. It's quite amazing and, as the film portrayed, the paths that you take where the light goes out, and where monsters seem to abound must be trusted for they will carry you to the place where you need to go (perhaps). I need to do a little more thinking about this but I do feel that we create much of our own unhappiness often by saying "no" to life.

Great Spirit. Wind blowing through my hair and across my face. Living earth beneath me. Life force all around me. Hold me and mine, and journey with us as we follow your various pathways. Help me to say "yes" to what is and thereby trust in the will of the universe, and in the magic of now.

* * *

We're driving to the Beltane ceremony, my son and I. We've just had a wonderful chat about all sorts of things. I've had to stop as I write this because I really don't want to forget what we chatted about. We talked about huge things like bullying. He agreed with me that the bullied victim is often a much stronger character than the archetypal bully, if he/she just stands his/her ground and refuses to be victimised. Of course, sometimes it's so hard to do that though. However, while one might not be able to show strength in a physical way, strength of character is often possible.

I told him that I've been bullied recently, through the church and outside it in everyday life. But I'm now stronger than those bullies because I will not be intimidated anymore.

We then talked about super powers and the ability to grant real wishes. For example, if you could possess any supernatural power, or if you were granted three wishes, what would they be? I genuinely had difficulty trying to think of what I'd ask for, not because there's so much to have but because I already have so much. I may be poor and live in a run-down ex-council house, but I feel rich inside. I am not depressed any more. Ok, I go through hard days and get dragged down by external pressures and human traumas, but by and large I'm happy and content within my deepest self. So I do not really want these major wishes because *magic* is here now in the moment, and the things I dream of are well on the way to materialising anyway.

A few years ago I had so many future wishes. I hated my life. Now, however, all is different! I once dreamed of being a writer (full-time). I once dreamed of being a magician (full-time). Both have become reality through the mess and crap of following an inner compulsion to be true to myself.

* * *

Beltane was beautiful. To be there at a real Druidic festival again was very special. It was also just over a year since I'd taken my son, daughter and their friend to the very same place for the celebration of Imbolc. My son loved being there again this year. He seems to be a natural Druid and it was amazingly special to have him there. He took part in the ritual wearing his new robe looking like a little Hobbit. At one point the tribe's chief came round the circle, holding forth the Beltane fire (lamp) inviting us all to offer a word of wisdom or hopeful anticipation for the year ahead. The first person he went to was my own son and, for a moment, I caught myself getting a little concerned *oh shit what's he gonna do? Will he be embarrassed or put off by this?* I know what I'd have done if I'd have been put in the same position at the age of 12! But then again I never would have been in that position at the age of 12. I was too busy nicking booze from my granddad's garage and getting my mates drunk.

The chief gently asked my son, "Do you have anything to say for Beltane? Any words of wisdom?" To my utter astonishment (and delight) my son lifted his head, and declared, *"Live life, be true to yourself, and never be just what others expect you to be."* "Hail to the wisdom," came the enthusiastic response from the members.

I remember a time when a Baptist Minister criticised me after I declared that children can be genuinely wise. It was in a situation where we'd all been taught that wisdom is a gift that comes with age and that no one begins to learn real wisdom until after the age of 30. I said that children often amaze me by their wisdom and the Baptist Minister replied, "Mark, sometime we must have a conversation about the difference between wisdom and intuition."

I wish he'd have been at this circle and heard my son's words. No, Mr. Baptist; this WAS wisdom, wisdom that we could all do with. *"Live life, be true to yourself, and never be just what others expect you to be."*

I was then asked to bless and hand around the Beltane bread (another guy was to do the same with the horn of wine). It was another powerful moment. I walked up to the two fires at the centre of the circle and picked up the "Patten" of bread and rice cakes. I didn't really know what to say so I modified the Eucharistic offertory prayers and it all felt really appropriate:

Blessed are you, god and goddess of all creation
Through your goodness we have this bread to share
Fruit of mother earth and work of human hands
It will be for us a sign of nature's goodness and our spiritual unity
Bless it and us as we share these gifts

Then nature's magic responded for, near the end of the ceremony I heard that now very familiar guttural "honk" coming from above and, as I looked, I saw the beautiful black raven flying off. These rare birds, birds that I'd never seen until two years ago and which I thought I'd have to travel far to catch sight of now seem to follow me where ever I go. Yesterday, while gardening, a raven flew over me again. They seem to visit my house daily now. When I think back to when I first began writing my Blue Raven book, I'd never actually seen one in the wild. I longed to find a place in the UK where I could go and see some. *And now they come to me!*

* * *

I've just met the author and symbologist Adele Nozedar in Hay on Wye, after she was put in touch with me by Philip Carr-Gomm. We clicked immediately as we chatted over a bowl of soup. We talked about all things metaphysical. At one point we were talking about synchronicities and how the raven has appeared and spoken at various significant points (like up at the woods near the readings chair) and Adele told me that she's written a book on the secret language of birds. Then I said, *"I can see one now,"* as a huge blue lorry came down the street towards us with the image of a massive raven-like flying bird on the front. We looked at each other, beaming.

She then took me to her glorious little esoteric book shop/tarot reading parlour called Spellbound. Finally we went along to the Mothers' Union meeting where I'd been invited to perform. I asked Adele and some of her friends to come too. What an interesting mix, the Mothers' Union and a handful of esoteric Pagan locals including King Richard the King of Hay. It turned out to be a fabulous meeting and a huge crossover of spiritual/religious cultures. I even did a little astrological/tarot-type reading as part of my talk/demonstration. The Mothers' Union members *loved* it.

* * *

I'm off to meet author Gill Edwards and magickal scholar Marcus Katz on the weekend. I can't wait. Another turning point maybe? Who knows?

* * *

My newest book, *Jesus through Pagan Eyes*, will (I now know) not just be on how Pagans see Jesus but also on what nuggets of light there are in his story that can be enlightening *for* Pagans. It will not seek to influence in a religious way, but will try to reclaim some of the more useful Jesus wisdom and add it to the universal story. For example I now call some of the failure-restoration stories of Jesus' life (in a slightly facetious way) *sin*-chronicities; in other words necessary "sins" that occur at exactly the right time. Perhaps Judas' action was one such *sin*-chronicity. The prodigal son is a universal story of *sin*-chronicity.

Some very weird synchronicities are occurring at the moment. Today's been very stressful. My head has been all over the place, quite out of touch with reality; racing, chasing, resenting, fighting. So I decided to have a hot bath before getting the kids' lunch.

I sank down in the hot soapy water and began reading Eckhart Tolle's book, *A New Earth*. It's quite remarkable. I love his writing. He manages to speak with a tone of Eastern wisdom, yet in a real and earthy way. He begins by talking about the evolution of plants and their eventual flowering. He sees the flowering of plants as their own enlightenment. He also sees the Buddha and Jesus as enlightened masters who advised their own disciples to study or gaze at flowers. The essential message of the book is that the human mind seems to have a deep dissatisfaction (an ego) which is a certain kind of insanity or madness. All this causes suffering, dukkha. The suffering stems from the mad human mind. Our human minds, in other words, are the cause of all our problems. We need to wake up out of the illusions caused by the insane and sleeping human mind.

And, just then, as I was lying there, still stressed, still pissed off, still very much in my own pathetic head (or the illusion of it) and reading these wisest of words, as if by magic a huge droplet of cold water formed itself into a great ball above me and fell from the shower right onto my forehead. The shower had not been switched on, or used at all, yet now it was sending me droplets of refreshing water, *splash!*

Gosh, that was good timing, I thought to myself, as the cold droplet ran down my face waking me out of a drowsy depressed slumber. Then there came another drop, and another, fresh cold water; and another still until it turned into a regular trickle. Then it seemed like someone had actually turned the tap full on. The water literally gushed out and poured all over my head for about a minute until it started slowing down again and finally stopped.

As I read on and allowed the water to refresh and awaken me, I noticed how Tolle alluded to how both Buddha and Jesus, in very different ways, attempted to *wake people up* to the deeper reality under all the maya/illusion of the ego. Jesus' term for such disconnection was "sin," a term misunderstood and misapplied by many. Funny how, only this morning, I'd been thinking about *sin*-chronicity.

* * *

I'm now sitting in Leominster Priory for the annual event of Mayor Making. I'm not the vicar any more but have been invited to perform some close up magic for the guests.

Walking into this place was odd and more than a little scary. Many ghosts still haunt my Priory vicar's past. However I was embraced and kissed by one of the very special ladies of this particular church as I entered. Helen Bricknell and her husband Geoff are warm and loving people. There are many beautiful souls there; Barbara Watkins, Shelagh Packwood, Dr. Clare Cathcart and others. And Mike, the vicar, always makes a special effort. He's a lovely guy and a good parish priest.

It's nice to be at these town events, but church services just don't work for me anymore. They are dull, wordy, heady and very male in tone. Give me a Beltane fire ritual any day. Church people really do need a good old dose of imaginative, spiritual, earthy Paganism.

I'm outside for a bit after receiving a phone call. It feels good to be out here with the wind blowing my hair and fresh drops of rain on my neck. Here I feel more in touch with what I am part of, at one with the deity that we do not attempt to encase within the rigid walls of buildings, books or bishops.

A bishop just rang me in fact. My ex-bishop phoned to say that he'd heard I was asked to perform an interment at a country church cemetery. He said he's also heard about my Christo-Pagan encounters and felt that this ruled me out from doing anything within a Church of England churchyard. I agreed to let the funeral director know. It had been a direct request from a family who'd used me for a "Catholic-yet-not-overly-religious" funeral ceremony held at the local Crematorium. I had told them I could only agree to the interment if I first had the permission of the local vicar. Apparently the local vicar in question did agree but then mentioned it at his local clergy chapter meeting and, after the discussion that followed, ended up with a strong recommendation that the whole matter be referred to the archdeacon (and that, of course, meant the bishop). The funny thing is that the family could have invited literally anyone to say some informal prayers at the side of the grave (which is all I would have been doing). Hell, I know plenty of funeral directors who do it themselves *and some of them are agnostic*. But me, a priest who has Druidic leanings, who would have been doing it not as a vicar but as an independent celebrant, was deemed inappropriate. Thinking about it, I imagine a first century rebellious Palestinian preacher/healer/story-teller would have evoked the same kind of knee jerk reaction were he to have been invited to do it.

* * *

Today I'm buzzing with excitement. I'm off to visit a part of the country I've never seen before, the Lake District! I'm also going to meet the author Gill Edwards and the Wiccan priest and tarot expert Marcuz Katz. How awesome.

I must say, after that recent funeral saga, I almost feel like publicly renouncing the church, my orders as a priest and the whole lot. If that is their attitude then do I ever really wish to be associated with them? BUT I will not renounce them. Why? Because I know deep down that the church is a frail, human institution. It's made up of flawed individuals who are (all of us) limited by the ego. And I'm one of them. How can I expect the church to be perfect when I'm so far from perfection myself?

I remember my wise friend James Fahey's words, *"Let them live their lives exactly as they choose."* In other words let it all go. Focus, rather, only on my own life, for that is all I have the right to do. I have no business at all trying to fix, control, change or influence anyone else, period! If people insist on demonising me, or stopping me doing things out of fear and control, then let them. I've met so many open, loving, peace-filled and thoroughly magical new friends over the last two years that I'm much better off in the true friend department anyway.

* * *

I'm sitting at the table of an Indian restaurant in Keswick after having spent an amazing day with Gill Edwards. We talked as we walked the fells and lakes, discussing all things spiritual and magical. Gill lives a truly authentic life *to the full*. Her story is inspirational. I have so much more to say about my new friend. I'll be back with her on Tuesday and Wednesday. One thing she really challenged me on was how I let my life be so manipulated by others, and also how I try to protect the people I love the most (like my children) from the truth by not letting them know the full story (*i.e. my side of the story*). I told her that I'm often scared of what such truth would do to them; scared of their reactions, scared of how it could potentially hurt their relationship with those they love (even though, it seems, this consideration never seems to come to be reciprocated). She said, *"I've never thought the truth is something to fear Mark."* Boy did that challenge me.

Gill's house is situated next to the poet Wordsworth's old home. It's quite a thought to think that he would have probably spent many hours in the house I'm staying in.

I've just had a call from Marcus Katz who's going to demon-strate a live tarot reading in the morning and then take me for a meal with a school RE Teacher in the evening; an RE Teacher who's also a tarot reader. *Freak Out!*

* * *

On the way up to Cumbria I heard an interesting radio programme on Iceland and their massive economic recession. However the encouraging news is that it has triggered a national recovery of their cultural food traditions. The interviewees were saying things like, *"On the positive side we are at last beginning to recapture a sense of what it means to be Icelandic. We are re-discovering who we are."* I thought *wow that is a nation's example of the Gospel of Falling Down, finding light through the cracks!*

* * *

I'm watching the news and the Speaker at The House of Commons is heading for trouble. Over the last week a huge scandal about MP's expenses has exploded onto the broad sheets and TV screens. Today (though this man was clearly some part of the problem, but only a minor part) it looks like the rest of the MPs have found an answer, something that might satisfy the national public demand for metaphorical blood. And here comes the use of the ancient scapegoat mechanism again. How satisfying, but how illusionary it all is. We get to feel better because he now represents our "sin" and he gets the chop so we now feel free, yet inside we are just as dark as him, because no inner transformation has happened. The Cross never did mean that. Jesus used the scapegoat imagery to prove once and for all how that is *precisely not* how God works. Yet we got it all totally back to front and ended up with a religion that can often be worse than the religiosity he came to challenge.

* * *

Sometimes modern spiritual gurus and wizards of pop psychology come out with the glossiest platitudes, all about health, success, being blessed by the universe (as almost a "divine right") and so on, and all from the comfort of very secure and pampered lives. What I so admire about Gill is that she is battling with cancer and living in a permanent state of loss (with regard to a relationship she cannot have because of circumstances) and yet lives life to the full. She walks, swims, reads, writes, eats properly and meditates. She's an inspiration to me, and a challenge to get my own health in order. I really do need to get all my priorities right, bodily and spiritually.

* * *

Marcus Katz has been fascinating. It's been so good to be immersed within the tarot world for a few days. I've gained so much wisdom and insight from this man of long experience.

The more I do tarot the more I feel that the cards map out not necessarily an objective picture of the situation but how the querant *sees* the situation. For example when I have been scared to ask certain questions I notice the "darker" cards tend to show up. Maybe, just maybe, for me, they reflect the fears, emotions and concerns themselves, rather than the specifics of the situation? If this is the case then it becomes more a counselling tool for getting people to take responsibility than a predicative oracle.

Marcus has been so helpful. His simple model (learned in 10 minutes) is quite brilliant and will now stay with me and develop. It is something I can practise even in the imagination by drawing certain cards mentally and meditating upon them. He also has a vast amount of knowledge about magick and the occult. It's been so good to listen to him talk about his views on Wicca, The Golden Dawn and Crowley et al.

Last night he talked about how the Western Mystery Tradition has been largely misunderstood as a tool for personal material gain, whereas in actual fact it holds the key to enlightenment, akin to Eastern Hinduism and Buddhism. He says the western religious world has been so incapable of leading people to enlightenment because of its dogma and control, and that the esoteric community has held it (the magick) in place of the mainstream denominations. This makes much sense to me.

* * *

The tarot experience was amazing and I even did a reading for Gill when I was back with her. I was quite nervous because I knew her situation was full of pain and longing and there are no easy answers. But incredibly the cards perfectly mapped out the place where she was in every way, also giving strong clues as to how to live with the situation. It also taught me not to fear the "dark" cards for the three "darkest" cards also came up in this spread, Death, the Devil and the Ten of Swords.

The night before coming home I asked a question of the cards regarding my book *The Path of the Blue Raven*. I drew the Tower (The Blasted Tower as Marcus Katz calls it), a destructive bolt from the blue. What was I expecting?

The very next morning the shit hit the fan. I had a phone call while on the way home, from one of the contributors to my book, a good friend of mine and a fellow priest. He'd written a beautiful piece for the book about Druidry through Christian eyes, but he told me that the local clergy were all frantic because of certain rumours about the book's contents. He was also worried that he might be caught up in any potential crossfire, because of his story being in the latter part of the book. One of the senior clergy suggested that he remove his story before it's published because he suspected it might make his own life very difficult!

It seems that clergy are a frightened species at the moment, and not due to persecution from the so called "enemy out there." They are frightened of people within their own church.

I tried to convince my friend that his words were really very orthodox and that there was absolutely no way anyone from within the church would be able to attack him over them. But it was not that that was the problem. It was simply the fact that he had written in a book authored by me, and I was seen as potentially dangerous.

By this time the book had been copy-edited and designed. It would be a nightmare to remove the chapter and may cost me a lot because of all the necessary re-numbering and setting. My friend's having a day to consider what to do. Well what a month May has turned out to be. How it all crumbles so easily.

* * *

Last night I took my son to the Wandmakers. Amazing. Two local hedge-witches I've discovered make the most beautiful wands, staffs and faery knives. And (just like in Harry Potter) the wand *chose* my son. He could feel it saying, "I'm yours" and it turned out to be made of Ash, his middle name.

* * *

I've just taken the decision out of my friend's hands (the fellow priest and contributor to my new book). I've arranged with my publisher to have his piece removed. God only knows how much it will cost me, but I really do not want to be responsible for making a fellow priest feel insecure. He was going to think about it, but I have decided. The chapter must be taken from the book.

* * *

Big decisions now plague my mind about whether or not to remain an ordained Anglican. Indeed, do I really still feel able to wear the label "Christian Priest" at all? But is it perhaps just the model of churchianity that's wrong? Is there another form that I could feel more part of? I need to seek advice.

* * *

Thank you my children, thank you mum, thank you Gerry, thank you Gill, thank you Caroline and thank you all the others who stopped me from making a huge mistake and going ahead with a renunciation of my orders as a priest. I'd convinced myself that to be truly authentic I must renounce them. My advisers all said "don't be so rash, wait, sleep on it, reflect, think more carefully." and they were right. I'm now listening to Fr. Matthew Fox via YouTube, and I can see that there really is a truly authentic, eclectic and nature-based way of understanding Christ and my own priesthood.

* * *

The new book I'm working on, *Jesus through Pagan Eyes*, has led me to some mind blowing email exchanges and phone conversations. I've just spoken to Maxine Sanders, the famous Witch Queen of the '60s and wife to the founder of Alexandrian Wicca, Alex Sanders. I'm going to be interviewing her for the book. She also put me in touch with a High priest, Scott Blunt, who has a deep and passionate love for Jesus and Catholicism.

Talking to Scott took my breath away, literally. Rarely have I heard Christians talk with such devotion about their saviour. And yet here was a Wiccan High priest coming to tears when speaking of his love for Jesus.

June

My dear "Brummy" priest friend's really concerned about me and my Pagan explorations. I wish she'd allow me to travel the path that I feel I need to walk and simply give me her blessing rather than her anxiety, or even to allow me to *be* the prodigal son for a while, if that's what she thinks I am. I'm so much freer and happier than when I was a vicar!

* * *

Last night was fabulous. I travelled to Leek in Staffordshire and performed my magic for a Church Mission Weekend. It went very well. Hundreds of people came to the town centre social club where it was held. The clergy were all very accommodating. I'd been to theological college with one of them, a guy called Karl. The format was this: my 45-minute act, break for food, comedian (Stuart), brief pause for cakes and coffee, and a round off with a word from the brilliant Bishop of Stafford, Gordon Mursell. He was fantastic I must say. Gordon is a warm and generous man with a relevant (and hilarious) message. I'd come across him a few times before, once at my own (ex) Diocesan Convention where he spoke on the Psalms in an engaging and comedic way. Then, only a few weeks ago, I'd performed in his company in Swanwick at the Leicester Diocesan Conference. Here in Leek we had the chance to sit and chat for a bit. We talked about magic and its ability to open folk up to wonder and deeper magical experiences. His final talk was absolutely great. He had the whole place with him; all those guys and girls (not churchy people) were eating out of his hands.

* * *

I'm off to Chelmsford tomorrow, to perform at the church of a vicar-friend who used to be a curate where my mother lives, Tupsley in Hereford. I'm really looking forward to it.

* * *

It did me good to meet such an open minded and friendly bishop last night. He even spoke to me about Pagans, saying he'd got two on one of his committees and how lovely they were.

* * *

Well I had a wonderful time in Chelmsford at Clare's church. She's a warm and caring priest!

* * *

Wow I've just had an incredibly moving and generous letter from a Church of England bishop saying that a "door's always open" should I ever wish to return. I'd shared my whole story with him! This is the second Anglican bishop who's basically given me a green light.

* * *

How weird. I've noticed that I've been "speaking in tongues" a lot lately. What's that all about then? I don't really believe in it! I've done it on and off for years (and don't honestly know why) but lately it's been there constantly. It takes me back to when I was a member of the Elim Pentecostal Church in Hereford. They used to teach that a sign of being "baptised in the Spirit" (or Spirit filled) was the ability to speak in tongues. It's an odd thing.

You just blurt out this strange gobbledygook that can sound like anything from a real human language to a baby's babbling. Some "words" are (in my opinion) subconsciously learned from hearing others do it because the same weird terms and phrases tend to become common. Some people in Elim saw it as the language of angels, and others saw it as a deep prayer language which actually means nothing in particular but expresses feelings and intentions in an ecstatic way. We used to joke that if it was the language of angels they seemed to be obsessed by *"calor gas heaters"* and must ride motorbikes because another couple of common phrases were *"she come on a Honda,"* and *"could have been a Kawasaki."*

Another idea was that this "language" was God speaking directly (prophetically) to his people but, because it was unintelligible, it required another person to interpret it. I remember being quite disappointed by the interpretations because they seemed so dull and obvious to be from the Creator of the Universe. One of my friends once did something quite terrible (but very funny) during a tongues and interpretation session. There was an old guy who used to talk (tongues) in a way that suggested the language of the Far East, perhaps Chinese or Japanese. He'd stand up and shout out, "Tokotah, takoto, chakulla, yazomazi" and so on. Anyway this one Sunday he'd done his thing and we all waited for the interpretation. Nothing came, so my friend stood up and declared, *"The Lord Saith, I'll have a number 45 and fried rice please."* Hilarious.

* * *

Well the Q and A interviews and articles for my new book are beginning to appear, along with the most unbelievably generous sentiments with regard to their not expecting any financial rewards. One lovely Druid author said, "We don't do it for the money but for the love of the gods." A Wiccan priest said, "Think of it as one author supporting another." I could not ask for more than that! I'm speechless.

* * *

I'm about to visit a family who've asked me to perform a naming ceremony for a little boy. I've parked a short way up the lane towards their house. It's exquisitely beautiful here. I can hear wildlife all around me (various kinds of birds and other animals). I can also hear the mystical sound of running water, a nearby stream perhaps?

Sometimes I find it hard to breathe when exposed to this kind of natural beauty. It's enchanting, like living magically and experiencing that all is one, everything is connected. I'm totally intoxicated by it. Great Spirit, gods, goddesses, energies, spirits of place and power. I breathe you into my body and feel your presence.

I was offered a way back into the church's official ministry today, parish ministry no less, yet I now know I cannot. I've travelled too far and have tasted too much of the Promised Land, where milk and honey flow freely. He was kind (the bishop who offered me the way back in) but I am now on a very different path.

I noticed my prayer had changed again when I knelt at my altar this morning. It has become much more meditative lately. I've dispensed with books for now, preferring to simply light my candles, incense and sit eyes closed in prayerful awareness of the divine presence.

* * *

I hadn't seen my raven visitors for a while, a few weeks at least, but this morning they called again. My head was buried in a research book and there they were soaring over my head, just letting me know that they are (and consequently God/dess is also) still with me.

I've been reading so much lately, from a whole variety of perspectives. My head is full and throbbing. I need to settle again, and allow myself to feel the peace, the mental rest of truly letting go and trusting in what is. Doubts, confusions, inner questioning and even those occasional bouts of fear, always cease when I stop and plug back into God/dess.

* * *

I've just spoken to world renowned Wiccan teachers, Janet Farrar and Gavin Bone. I'll go across to Ireland and interview them properly someday. They even invited me to stay. Incredible. This new project is a whole new magical adventure for me. The generosity of the folk I'm encountering is blowing my mind. Janet shared an experience that was profound and to do with the Holy Grail. Gavin said how the Grail stories used to be a bridge, a bit of common ground between Christians and Pagans. But that commonality is going now that younger Pagans are growing up without those myths.

* * *

How sad. I've just had a walk down *The Grange* and passed an angry old man from my old church. He just turned round, stood, and glared, shaking his head at me. I don't understand why people are sometimes so hostile and never seem to be able to let go. This poor chap and many like him have attended church every week of their lives, and yet it seems to have had no impact whatsoever on their characters. Alas, it is a mystery indeed.

* * *

Sometimes this attempt at a life of honesty and authenticity is so hard. The money I either lose or choose to turn down because I refuse to buy into the usual "tit for tat" system, makes life really crippling at times.

A clergy friend just phoned to warn me about my book *The Path of the Blue Raven* again, suggesting that I basically try to play it down and keep a low profile. He said he was concerned about what could still happen to me. I could still be vilified and seen as dangerous, therefore losing me the last remaining bit of respectability I have with the Christian world. I said that after everything I'd been through for the sake of integrity, how could I allow fears like that to control me?

We talked some more and I said how sad it was for clergy to be in such a prison that renders them ineffectual puppets. And he said (I could not believe it), "It's alright for you Mark. You have the luxury of being on the outside now!" To which I replied, "Yes, but please don't ever think it's a luxury. Look at what it cost, and look at what it still costs. My integrity still means that I live in such turmoil and near poverty at times. I have to refuse big offers that could carry me out of the mess, because *I HAVE* to be fully real, fully me, fully authentic. I refuse to hit back in a tit for tat way just to make a buck. I have even refused to sell the big potential press stories for money because I do not wish to dish out 'dirt for dirt.'"

When I got home and spoke with some of my family about it all, one of them snapped and shouted, *"Mark, face it. Your own spiritual family, Hereford fucking Diocese, don't give a shit about you. They've dumped you Mark. Face it they're not your fucking family."* I couldn't disagree.

* * *

It's the morning of the Summer Solstice. I'm up at 3am and now racing down the usual Gloucester, Swindon, Marlborough route, to one of the most magnificent and awe inspiring places on earth, *Stonehenge*. One of the extra blessings of being a member of *The Order of Bards, Ovates and Druids* is that, each year, the Order holds a summer solstice ceremony within the great stone circle itself. We are given permission to enter that awesome sacred sundial. It's a profound experience.

On this occasion something totally breath-taking took place. We made our way under the road tunnel in a long and colourful robed procession. I walked close to Keith, the Druid Chief of my local (Cornovii) group. He's a large man and was wearing a long white robe and carrying a huge sword. I smiled as we walked past a concerned looking group of tourists and, with a twinkle in his eye, Keith said loudly, "Aren't you going to join us for the sacrifice?"

We then paused outside the stone circle, a group of about 200 Druids, and "called the quarters," which means welcoming the spirits of the four directions (the compass points) and creating a sacred circle of space by moving round the circumference of the henge before entering its centre. When we were at the first point I noticed a little rabbit half hidden by the long grass and only a few feet away from us. I was amazed that it did not jump up and run away. When we started off for the second point, to my great surprise, the little creature raised itself up on its very long hind legs. It was not a rabbit at all, but a hare. Not only was this the first time I'd ever seen a wild hare, I also knew that it was one of the most significant creatures within Druidry and Paganism. It's the animal of the moon, and thus of the Goddess, and here it was among us. Indeed I'll never forget the fact that this magical hare actually walked right round the circle with us, pausing every time we stopped to call the quarters. It only decided to leave us as we finally entered the stone circle for the main part of the ceremony.

Once inside we were then joined by another animal, a little bird. Jackdaws are a feature of Stonehenge and one of them flew down and stood close to the Druid who led the ceremony. It was so wonderful to be joined by creatures of the earth and sky for our celebration of the Summer Solstice.

* * *

Something occurred to me quite powerfully this morning. When I was first initiated in a New Mexican desert by Richard Rohr, he advised us all of two things for the future:

1 Do not try to explain it to others. They will not understand and may even ridicule it.
2 Look out for synchronicities. They are likely to be more frequent.

These two points, now some eight years later, have just come to me as *beacons of light*.

Yesterday I was phoned by a friend who tried to advise me to reconsider my Blue Raven book. He was expressing his fear that the press might twist things to create a scandal. In the end I told him that I cannot let myself be a slave to that kind of fear again. The fact is that there are people who do not live with honesty and integrity. They cover up their own failures in an effort to climb to the top, or even to keep hold of the futile rubbish they have. And these people will *NEVER* be able to understand those who are willing to take the risk of being true to themselves. They, through the compulsion to hold onto their safe jobs and live "secure" lives, are bereft of magic and simply live inside disenchanted worlds. They say the "right" things but live without many of the adventures that come so frequently when you are plugged into true destiny.

The point I'm trying to make is that my first initiation (in that vast and hot New Mexican desert) *did* transform me. It took a good few years to recognise what was going on inside me but, once recognised, there was no turning back. My second (Druidic) initiation moved the process onwards even further and the two new books I'm writing now are a direct result of that. Incredible!

* * *

Things are moving on so rapidly with my writing. I've had two huge US publishers interested in my books now. I'm hoping that I'll soon get the official go ahead for *Jesus through Pagan Eyes*. On that note I've just heard from the amazing American Wizard Oberon Zell Ravenheart. He's now going to contribute too. How fantastic.

* * *

I love it when the local funeral directors phone me to ask questions about various problems or matters they ought to really phone their local clergy about. They know I've not been one for over two years but they still feel able to ask for my advice. I feel deeply privileged.

* * *

The *magic* of magic! In my work as a close up magician I do a date of birth playing card effect. Basically I get a spectator to take a card but not look at it. There's no force involved. It is a genuinely free choice. Then I ask for her date of birth and work out, from the star sign and numerology, what the card is. It occurred to me years ago that the four suits relate to the four elements and therefore to people's zodiac signs. All you need to do is to work out which element the suit is and convert it to tarot. For example diamonds in tarot are pentacles or coins, which represent the element of earth and the zodiac types Capricorn, Taurus and Virgo.

Today someone snatched the cards from me as I was doing this favourite effect of mine. She said, "Right let me do it to you then; if it really works then it'll work now." I had just got her card exactly right. She was the 13th March. Her card was 4 of hearts. 1 + 3 (from the 13th) adds together to make 4. March is Pisces and therefore cups/hearts.

So then she tried to do it to me. And, amazingly, after I'd I told her my date was March 8th she revealed that my card was indeed the 8 of hearts. I *love* it when real magic happens.

* * *

This is the weekend of the actual Summer Solstice (a week later than the OBOD Stonehenge gathering). I used it as an opportunity to take stock and say goodbye to some of the bad habits I'd allowed to develop (primarily over eating and drinking badly). I was amazed at how powerful an experience it was. I stood, looking out at the fields and hills, and used an OBOD solo ritual invoking the sun god.

I asked for strength to make this pivotal point in the year a time of letting go of all the bad habits that hold me back, psychologically, spiritually and emotionally. I could not believe the energy I sensed from God. I have recently discovered a new dimension to the mother aspect of deity, the divine feminine. It is a facet of the divine that I guess I have never had a problem connecting to; the loving, nurturing, unconditionally grace-filled, dark, psychic aspect of the divine. The problem I had in the past was not that I do not understand a feminine face of God but that I never had a language to express it. My Catholic Marian flirtation helped but it was not until I met the Pagan Goddess that I found a language of expression for this God (dess) I already knew.

And today I sensed a definite male God energy, the sun god of light, warmth, fertility, strength and fire. I felt him and he complemented the mother goddess on whom I stood (earth). I am becoming more holistic spiritually.

* * *

I'm back in my study and I don't believe it. I heard a noise, *RAVEN*. Two of them flew over and landed in the huge tree just outside my window.

* * *

I have just dropped my daughter off at her first day of college. All grown up. I'm so very proud of her. I also popped into the church where I first served as a deacon.

* * *

How beautiful to have conducted my first ever Druidic baby naming ceremony. Little Eli is a sweet two year old boy with wonderful open-minded and devoted parents. We had Pagan-themed nature readings, blessings of the elements and lots of magic. We also had god and goddessparents.

* * *

I'm watching a TV programme called Revelation, how to find God! It's about the Alpha Course. It was not very convincing at all. In fact it seemed that "conversion" was almost happening in the other direction. An agnostic candidate's questions really challenged one of the leaders who ended up having a tantrum.

What was really interesting was that the one of the more experiential sessions was far more successful than the theoretical sessions with regard to discussion. It was simply a two-minute silence and then a chat about how or what happened.

I found the "Holy Spirit Weekend" highly unsettling and quite disturbing. The vicar had unfortunately and unwittingly set up a hypnotic hook by saying something along the lines of "the Holy Spirit is gentle like a dove and a loud noise could scare him away." Then, a little later, when the vicar led a quiet time for inviting the Holy Spirit in, a great noise erupted outside. Sports cars started up, and revved loudly making it quite impossible to relax or stay with the spirit inside the room. It totally broke the spell.

My hunch is that genuine spiritual experiences can and do occur through such events as this but that the particular form of the mythology is actually irrelevant. It could just as easily happen within the context of a Catholic retreat or a Hindu temple. One really off-putting thing was when the vicar said, "I can thoroughly recommend the Holy Spirit. Why don't you give Him a go?" This was in reference to being "baptised in the spirit." Horrible! It sounded like an advert for an alcoholic drink.

* * *

I've noticed my prayer changing again. I kneel at my altar to God/dess and now tend to use no words at all, or few. I don't feel like I'm worshipping either. I simply kneel and take in the now, the presence of the spiritual world, the Mother and Father of us all. I simply soak it all in. My prayer is becoming quite Eastern.

* * *

I'm nervous today. I have to attend my old church, *the Priory*, for a funeral. I'm doing the "Green" part up at Humber Woodland

Burial afterwards. Mike, the vicar, is a good man and wanted me to be part of the church part too, so I'm going to sit in the congregation and he'll mention that I'm there.

* * *

I'm now sitting in the lady chapel after having met some of the church helpers coming in. It was really lovely to see them. They were friendly and welcoming. I also lit a candle at the votive stand which has a gorgeous Icon of Our Lady of Taize. She still moves me, this Mary the Theotokos, the God Bearer. I wonder why?

I sit in the lady chapel and see images of her everywhere. Perhaps Mary the human mother of the human Jesus has actually become a Mother Goddess in her own right? She certainly seems to have a presence, a personality. I am communicating with her too! She is an image of deity just as Jesus is, and just as the god images of other religions are.

Now I'm sitting in the main nave of Leominster Priory. I face the "infamous" St. Paul's chapel over which so much metaphorical blood was spilled during my time here. When I think back to that saga it sends shivers down my spine. To cut a very long story short it was to do with an expensive new piece of furniture for the chapel, a semi-circular set of benches and a central altar; a gift to the church for the New Millennium. But the resistance was immense, with so much back stabbing and underground manipulation by some of those against. A feature of the altar was that it was *circular* and we were amazed that some of those against it claimed it was to be a business meeting table and therefore the chapel would cease to have a spiritual function at all, while others said it was Pagan. It ended up being installed years after the actual Millennium has passed. "See how these Christians love one another!"

I now sit and gaze at the altar, the sacred table where I shared so many meals, so many "feasts of heaven." I can visualise all the beautiful experiences when I'd invite the children to come and stand round the altar. I think of the Midnight Masses when the non-church community would enter in and be welcomed on a frosty winter night. They always brightened up the place.

As I sit and reflect I wonder *am I still a priest*? In a strange kind of way I can quite easily imagine standing there now and celebrating communion. I truly felt Jesus and Mary's presence here today and I even found being there quite emotional. I think it was the experience of connectedness, that we are all one. I still feel like I should hold onto my priesthood and not throw it all away just yet. I hear myself saying, *"You may hate churchianity Mark, but churchianity is not what Jesus is about."*

July

I'm on the way to Manchester, to perform at St. George's Church Stockport. I'm really looking forward to it. I still love visiting churches and sharing my magic with them. Yes I do still feel I'm some sort of priest. It's just that I don't go in for all the *stuff* anymore. It clutters everything.

I'm listening to the radio and had to stop to write this down. The Church of England has formed yet another intolerant new group, this time to do with re-claiming "true biblical authority." It's obviously anti-gay. A bishop member was quoted saying, "we welcome homosexuals; we just want them to repent and change."

* * *

I'm sitting in the lady chapel of the beautiful St. George's Stockport and I've decided to do a spiritual/theological review and ask myself some questions on where I am within all this Christian and Pagan muddle, and whether there's any harmony between the two traditions.

1 What is God/Deity?
God is source, the ultimate source of love, creativity, spirit, oneness, beauty - manifested throughout "creation." God is both male and female creative energy, God and Goddess. God is both immanent and transcendent. So far all the above is appropriate for both a Christian and a Pagan.

2 Who was/is Jesus?
Jesus was an enlightened human who was so aware of his god-self that he became a "god" to others, not for them to fall down and worship him but to point the way to the god-self inside each

one of them. Thus Christianity fails when it causes barriers to develop between us and the divine. The Buddha was very similar to the one we call The Christ. Both were fully human individuals who gained enlightenment, total self-knowledge. They were both made aware of the essential fact of their divine state. Both were given titles "The Buddha," "The Christ." Buddha helps us awaken our Buddha nature. Christ helps us discover our Christ-consciousness. So far all this can be believed by both a Christian and a Pagan.

Jesus died (was murdered) not as a divine sacrifice but because he threatened both "church" and "state." He threatened religion by making it superfluous. He pointed to the one-ness that already exists between the divine and the material worlds (us). Temple structures and priesthoods that perpetuate a "separated universe" need to remember this.

The character of Jesus then had the usual legends and myths built up around him, which all add to the essence *if seen as myth* but which ruin the story when literalised.

3 What is Christianity – the central truths?

If every religion has a major gift which I believe they do, then what is Christianity's gift to the world? I believe it is the Christ image of a god being plunged into raw, messy, sinful, human, broken life. He is a powerful symbol of a divine connectedness to all things, *even the shit*.

4 What about Nature Spirits/Fairies?

When I walk in a forest I don't need to *believe* that spirits are there. I *know* they are. I feel them. I can sense the energy, the magic. Nature is a beautiful gift of magic. Fairies exist I believe. I believe that they are the energy that hums and pulsates throughout all living and non-living matter. Funnily angels (in some parts of the Judeo-Christian world) come across as "nature spirits." We each have a guardian angel, so the Christians myth says. Thus, once again, there need be no real contradictions between Druidry and Christianity here.

5 What about church buildings?

As I sit inside this Great Manchester Church, I can sense the love and devotion of the ancients who built it, and the many modern day souls who lovingly upkeep it. It is indeed a sacred place, made sacred by the prayers and rituals of the centuries. In this sense it is no different to any churches, temples, mosques or gurdwaras, holy places, special places of magic and wonder.

* * *

What a moving experience! I just had tears in my eyes. The church was filled with happy, smiling, children's faces. Amazing. I miss this aspect of the vicar's role. I was given so much gratitude afterwards from all sorts of people and of every age. I really do see this as my ministry to the church now.

* * *

I've just sent emails to every single Diocese about my "Soulful Magic." I really feel I have something special to offer churches/Christians.

* * *

How tragic. A friend of a friend has been given news of terminal cancer. His wife phoned and asked me whether I'd go and plan his funeral with him. Sadly, they want it to be in the priory and I can't do it there. I'm not allowed to. My hands are tied.

* * *

Why?

I recently spent an entire day working on some new publicity and promotional material to send out to every Diocese throughout the whole Church of England. I emailed every Diocesan Office, as well as a fair few other people who I figured would be interested. It was a very positive piece of marketing with many church-based endorsements supporting what I do. But now, quite out of the blue, I have learned that a dose of negative campaigning has also been sent out about me. Someone sent out an email about me to the very same Diocesan officials I'd contacted to *counteract my own*. I've had a booking in the diary for over a year that may now be cancelled because of this negative publicity; a huge event at Canterbury Cathedral. Apparently the counteracting letter has already reached the chap who booked me. This is sure to be yet another sleepless night of which I just don't need.

* * *

To try to gain a little perspective I've come down to my spot at *The Grange* for a few minutes. Oh my word, three huge ravens just flew gracefully over my head. Beautiful. What perfect timing. Amidst all the turmoil caused by humans God sends his/her animal messengers to soothe our troubled minds.

* * *

This is turning out to be quite wonderful. I'm sitting in my car after just having met Peter Owen Jones.

I have to say, the guy really shook me. I had been feeling kind of "all over the place" after my recent episode of negative emails. His advice was to try to create some distance between me and them (the officialdom of the C of E). He advised not to be unloving but to simply recognise that me and they are in a different world now. He was intensely affirming and promised me his support. And then he invited me to say the Eucharistic Prayer in his own church on the Sunday morning.

Can I really? I have no license, yet he has invited me to. This guy puts his money where his mouth is. He also said it is possible to inhabit both spaces, i.e. to be both a Christian and a Druid. I have to ask myself which part of the Jesus/Christ story can I still make meaning out of. Can I really say the Mass? I can if I see the death of Christ as the murder of a radical who tries to give away the Gift of God in all. I can if the meal is symbolic of the cup we all take if we wish to follow. I can if it is a sharing in divine life! Why not?

I don't need to worry any more. I really don't. It's all becoming so much clearer now. I am still a liberal priest a post-denominational priest and pastor. And I am also a follower of the Druidic path. I am not a Christo-Pagan so much as a Christian and a Druid.

* * *

What an amazing experience! I'm now with Philip and Stephanie Carr-Gomm at the sixtieth birthday party of a famous Caribbean poet John Agard. James Berry, Grace Nichols and other poets and artists are also here. We are all being treated to a wonderful array of poetry and music from the guests.

Philip and I were chatting and he told me about how, apparently, when a mother is about to give birth, it is the baby itself that triggers the event. The baby apparently secretes something which makes the environment toxic and so, basically, what was (for nine months) a place of security, safety, warmth and "home," becomes a place of toxicity.

That is such a powerful metaphor for my current situation. The environment where we are nurtured, supported, held, fed and made secure sometimes needs to let us go, in order to not let us stagnate or be poisoned. And so sometimes we ourselves trigger a reaction; we do something that makes the whole place of security toxic! And so we have no option but to get the hell out! It's not that the environment becomes bad, evil or wrong, and neither do we. It's simply that, in order to grow, we must leave.

It's like the Prodigal Son. Incredible!!!

* * *

Today I'm travelling to Chester Cathedral. I've been invited to lead two huge (church-based) leavers' events for school children, and then one at a school near Liverpool too.

I definitely still seem to have a role within the church world, for those who feel they can cope with me. I'm in a place called Astbury, staying in the gigantic seventeenth century rectory.

* * *

I've just walked into Chester Cathedral, possibly one of the warmest, most colourful and gloriously inviting of all English cathedrals. The gorgeously rich stained glass, pink/grey stone and many words of welcome in various foreign languages take your breath away. I walked right in and wept! Something about it (in fact cathedrals in general) just moves me so deeply. So powerful.

So, here I am once again reminded of my link to the Anglican tradition and my own priesthood. I am beginning to realise that I can move within and plug into many spiritualities. I am still a priest, a Christian priest, and here I sense that calling again.

And I am also a Druid. I was with Philip yesterday, chanting the Awen standing round an oak tree. I sensed that calling there. Perhaps this whole Christo-Pagan quest is actually futile. Maybe I don't need to try to mix the two, or be half of each. Maybe I can be fully Druid and fully Christian?

Someone I met at John Agard's party told me that it is possible to be dual faith. He was Indian and said that many Indians have more than one religion. He said he was both Muslim and Taoist. Likewise Peter Owen Jones said the same. He can now live in more than one space with no conflicts of interest etc. Here may lie the way forward?

* * *

I've just bumped into Trevor Dennis the vice Dean of Chester. I could have wept. He gave me a huge hug and a smiling welcome. It was so good to see him again! He endorsed my first book and has been a constant source of support ever since.

To sit here now, on an Anglican platform and look out at 1,000 young smiling faces is amazing! Truly amazing.

* * *

Today it's the same thing (a school leavers' service) but this time held at the parish Church of Astbury. I stayed the night with a delightful clergy couple, Jonathan and Ella and their incredibly bright daughter Annie. They were very kind and gave true hospitality in their seventeenth century mansion of a vicarage. When I left their home Ella melted my heart. She came and said goodbye, but brought tears to my eyes with her embrace, kind words, and an invitation to visit again.

I simply *have* to find a way staying with all my own treasure, yet making what I do sensitive and safe for all those I have the privilege of meeting through the church. Thank you God.

* * *

Sometimes things just take my breath away! Today I opened an email, the sender's name of whom I didn't at first recognise; Steven Critchely. It rang a bell but only a vague memory. Then the penny dropped. It said, *"Dear Mark you have recently sent an email to someone I know and it came via my own mail. I think we know each other."*

Approximately 23 years before, he and I had been together in Belgium on a Pentecostal evangelistic mission. He was *the* one among our group that I really got on with. He was a very committed Pentecostal and, after the mission, both of us went off to do evangelistic things in different ways. Steve ended up working with big name evangelist Rhinehart Bonke's missions. *He now runs a Wiccan coven as the High priest.*

* * *

It's Saturday and I've just driven from Leominster to Tunbridge Wells and have noticed that I'm but a stone's throw from where I was last week with Philip Carr-Gomm. I'm here for an open air church-based community event. Last night I was performing at the Presteigne Sheep Music Festival situated on the Welsh border. I'm there again tomorrow. This afternoon I drive up to Nottingham for a friend's wedding. Busy life.

This month has been quite astonishing with regard to my faith. I've been finding myself more able to balance my Christian side with my Druid/Pagan side. Peter Owen Jones really helped me to see how I can be both. I do not need to choose and I do not need to mix them either.

* * *

It looks like my new book idea has "sold it" with Llewellyn. The acquisitions editor has emailed me to say how excited they all were with the proposal. So it's onto the contract and then comes all the hard work.

* * *

My right knee's really hurting. I think all the driving has put a huge extra strain on what is already a weak joint.

I've had X-rays recently but keep finding myself unable to check on the results. There's a loose joint and a feeling of grinding inside my knee. Oh well I'm here now at the end of the next stage of this, my biggest drive in one day; from Leominster, to Tunbridge Wells, to Nottingham and back to Leominster.

August

I'm at a certain Diocesan Retreat House leading a few days on my book *The Gospel of Falling Down*. I love coming here. They often invite me back but I think they might be making a loss this time. Sadly only four people have come, all elderly women. It may be because it's mid-week and hard for people to get to? Anyway, at least it's given me some time for reflection.

* * *

Things have been quite messy again lately. I missed the celebration of Lammas and I've not jogged or meditated for a few weeks. It's an up and down life this spirituality thing. Maybe something will come out of my experience of being here this time? I still can't fully work out where I'm supposed to be? Where is my spiritual home?

Mark, little brother, son, friend, saviour.

Saviour of yourself.

Listen now.

Hear the quiet; the quietness without and within.

Don't try to work it out.

Be, relax, listen, be aware, fall into pace with the pulse and gentle rhythm of life.

Love, love all, love yourself as you are, with all your unworked out questions and problems that keep you up at night.

Listen, and be prepared to lead others into that deafening silence, the silence that is the OM/AUM, the deep hum of the cosmos.

Everything, everything adds to that hummmmm.

Every squeak of the door, the turning of the pages of the books you read.

So now drift deeper, deeper into the awareness of what is, and trust it, fall inward.

Fall don't climb, rest don't toil, sink don't swim against the current.

For here, now, today, in this place, in you, is the gold, and the glittering gemstone of glory.

Yes it's often sought elsewhere, but it's never found out there.

Peace, let peace be part of you, breathe, breathe in the now-ness of today. Don't look for tomorrow. Don't search the future. Leave all thoughts of "there" and all questions of "where" and fix rather on "here."

* * *

It was lovely to have a few words with the brilliant priest-manager of this Diocesan Retreat House. He's a very open minded and inclusive guy. He impressed me last time with his open minded approach and his appreciation of the Pagan spirit.

* * *

Drat. I've just been sitting in the retreat house library reading so many of the academic and theological works I myself chucked out after I had to leave the vicarage in 2007. They would have been so useful now what with all the research I'm doing for a new book. Thousands of pounds' worth of books, all given away. Oh well I try to hold on to the notion that "nothing is wasted."

I just had the most profound discussion. The ladies were keen to fit in an extra session so we met for an hour before tea. Oh the conversation. Sometimes this is just such an awesome privilege. One of them really opened up about her life and living with herself for so many years, the depression, inner pain, and how to live with it. I felt so humble, so tiny, to be listening to such deep and powerful sentiments and experiences being expressed!

* * *

I'm now leading a meditation where we write a letter to God, and then a letter back to ourselves.

My Letter to God:

Source of all.
What's happening?
Why the confusion?
Why do I still continue to make life so difficult for myself?
I am so blessed, so free, so spiritually rich, yet still can't grasp who I am or even who you are!
There are so many contradictions.
There is so much I don't understand.
I don't know where I belong anymore.
I can't see a way to a community where I can grow/develop/explore.
I still love Jesus but find his church so hard, even meaningless at times.
I love the Druid path but still feel drawn to a great God/dess, a holding, healing, loving presence.
Where has my Jesus gone?
Where is he now?
Who is he now?
Can I still somehow follow you, Jesus, and also continue my Pagan journey?
What is the way for me now?
Please guide me.
What is my new calling?
I still love you!

* * *

The women I'm with here are truly inspirational. One is living with cancer. The other three have all lost their husbands, and all four have clearly used their remaining years to follow a deep spiritual journey. They are all so amazing. One of them was telling me of how she can "leave her body" and how she has done so right throughout her life (because life has itself been so unbearably awful at times). She said, "I know it's wrong. I know I shouldn't do it ... but."

I invited her to explore the reasons why part of her is telling the other part why it's wrong!

So, yet again, this retreat (like all others) gives me a glimpse into the depth of other people's lives. Such a profound privilege.

The four women just shared their letter to themselves. What each one came up with was truly incredible. The one that stood out was the ex-vicar's wife who simply cannot let go or allow herself to think it's ok to just enjoy herself for the sake of pleasure alone. There is so much "ought" in her words (she reminded me of myself). She said, "I know I *ought* to let myself off the hook a little more, and so many priests, counsellors, spiritual directors, tell me so, but I just *can't* seem to." I told her that the last thing I wanted to do was add to all that pressure and give her yet another "ought"- i.e. "you ought to be kinder to yourself" for that would be a contradiction in terms. Then she read out her little letter and heard herself saying something she could not believe she'd actually written. She heard herself saying that she was, "not all bad" and this little phrase was a ray of light for her. She admitted that she had not wanted to partake in the exercise because she thought it was "dangerous," but she did it anyway.

It was amazing! She'd said that her life had been easy (even cushy) and that she'd never had any reason not to believe in God. And how He'd always been there for her, yet that she could have done a whole lot more for him. Then she told me how life, since the '50s, had been one problem after another and how some problems had been extremely severe. She lost her husband young, and lost her parents at the same time, which (because her husband was a vicar) meant she lost her home *and role too.* She also lost her health, but she said she'd never considered any of that to have been hardships. However, in this letter she now realised that her life *had* been hard and that she *had* actually done extremely well to hold on to God through it all. "Maybe I haven't been so bad," she said, "Maybe I didn't need to go off and become a missionary in Africa. Maybe I've done ok!" Then she looked at me and, with a big beautiful smile, said, "Thank you Mark."

* * *

It's now lunch time and I'm totally shattered by how things can so suddenly change! We've been sharing the deepest aspects of human living on this retreat! We've all experienced waves of self-forgiveness and healing love. Tales of each of us playing the prodigal son, the failed priest, the broken servant of Christ, all in need of divine mercy. Yet, *crash*, at the dinner table I told them a little story about one of my best friends, a wonderful Roman Catholic priest who made the mistake of having a brief gay relationship a few years ago. The poor guy has not worked since then because his Archbishop sacked him.

And how did these women respond? They suddenly started defending the church hierarchy. They said that, because of the sake of keeping a good public appearance, the church needs to be harder on the "priests who've gone astray."

The conversation moved onto other forms of hierarchical hypocrisy and I told them how I was once advised (by a vicar) that it's always a good thing to be *seen* to be praying at the high altar before a service. "What's wrong with that?" said one of them.

The discussion continued and I said that Jesus himself seemed to ooze love and forgiveness to the most broken, fallen, sinful souls and "if only the hurch could reflect that a little more."

One of the women said, "Well if you don't like it, maybe you shouldn't be in the church." I didn't say (though maybe I should have) that I'm not actually "in" the church anymore because I took so seriously the need to confess my sins and play the prodigal son. And that not only did I not have a ring or robe or fatted calf but had everything taken away from me in the process.

The silliest phrase, and one which I'll never forget, was this. I'd just lamented that Jesus never seemed to act like modern day bishops and church leaders, because he always tended to forgive and look for reconciliation rather than punishment. I said that he certainly never seemed concerned about public appearances or respectability. At that one of the woman said, "Well it was easy for Jesus. He never had a church to run."

One tends to give up at points like this!

* * *

I'm at The Big Chill, a huge 40,000 person rock festival, with my son Jamie. I performed to an all age audience and an amazing synchronicity occurred. I did my effect called *Gemstone Colours*, where I get four volunteers to represent each of the four elements and imagine they're holding a coloured gemstone of their choice. I then work out what the colours are. One girl was called Tara and I said, "You must be green because your name reminds me of the Buddhist Goddess of compassion the Green Tara." Then, after the show a guy came up to me and said, "Wow, I love all your synchronicity stuff and the way you use magic to talk about spirituality and non-attachment stuff!" Then he showed me his arm, a huge tattoo of the Green Tara.

* * *

I'm now sitting in a place of indescribable beauty, just north of Tring in Berkshire. I'm about to officiate at a wedding and handfasting, in a forest!

The forest is incredible. It's utterly stunning. I've just taken a walk into the heart of it. This will be my very first wedding since June '07's departure from the church. And what a place for a first wedding. I've had a new clerical stole (scarf) made, one that shows the symbols of many faiths/paths.

My book *The Wizard's Gift* seems to foresee a time when the forest would be my cathedral. I've now done open air baby namings, woodland burials and now this amazing wedding blessing in an enchanted forest.

* * *

I felt moved to write a poem. I've called it *The Road*.

This road we walk,
An oft tangled web of trap and snare,
Created largely by our own unsettled minds,
Planning and grasping,
Regretting and denying,
Climbing the ladder,
Inching towards our goals that never come,
Aching for life to begin,
STOP!
Look down from the dizzy heights,
Who's at the bottom?
Who looks up with tear stained eyes and kisses that stretch through
*   time and space?*
YOU do - the YOU that "you" have forgotten,
The YOU that "you" left back there in what is actually NOW,
And so who is the "you" that has climbed so high and so far away
*   from YOU?*
Ah he/she is the "you" of tomorrow's dream,
And in reality is a mere illusion,

Yet so seemingly real and so seemingly powerful
STOP!
Look down,
Let go,
DROP!
And be caught and taught by YOURself,
For that is also where God/dess lives,
And that is where true life is lived,
TODAY - HERE - in the PRESENT,
. FALL back to NOW and taste the magic of the moment!

* * *

As part of my research for my new book I ventured the awesome Warwick Castle and visited their amazing dungeons, together with the "Heretic" experience. I saw the fearful instruments used on witches or heretics to extract confessions:

- Tongue stretchers
- Penis choppers
- Horrible hooks from which folk would be hung from the eye socket, base of neck or even anus.
- Jaw crushers
- Flesh gougers

* * *

I've been doing a little more theological thinking about the cross. I've always found the cross of Jesus a helpful image. I still wear two of them. Of course I can't cope with the "his blood washes away my sins" stuff but, rather, I see it as a deep and powerful symbol of the cost of being true to one's own deepest inner call/vocation. For Jesus (the man not the God) it was impossible for him not to offer grace to those to whom religion and politics had given the finger. It was what he knew deep down to be the way, to welcome the un-welcomeable, to love the un-loveable. That's why I can't buy the idea that Jesus was an Essene either. I mean, those guys were the strictest perfectionists in the area. They wouldn't have even visited regular people, let alone allowed fallen women to kiss their feet or touch lepers. They made the Pharisees look like liberals.

Jesus was doing something new. He even parted company with his own teacher/leader John the Baptiser and took the gift of grace into the towns and back-alleys from the desert, saying things like "come to me all who thirst."

And as he welcomed them (the ones at the edge and way outside the box) so he also put his own head on the block with regard to those who ran the boxed up system, those who'd created religious boxes for the "pure" and "worthy" and who held down the lid tightly by sitting down on top.

And as his popularity grew so he became more and more of a threat to the tight-buttocked establishment. But even knowing this, he continued undeterred by the reality of what may happen. He died for the sake of love and compassion (not unlike dear Gandhi). His rebellion was simply that he chose to say, in the words of the latter day saint Jeffrey Lebowski (from the Coen Brothers' film The Big Lebowski, and a definite Dude in his footsteps), "fuck it" to the high and mighty, and do his own thing man.

His was a gentle rebellion. No guns. No ultra-left wing terrorism. No holier than thou attacks. Just a simple refusal to be controlled from above and a brave and daring mingling with the messed and muddled up section of society, where he could lovingly give back some of the treasure that had been stolen by the big men who ran the show. Yet it cost him everything!

And I (as a pretty lame follower of this first century Dudely hero) now wear the image of his death with pride. Oh I hate what they (the new messengers of boxed up religion) did with it to be sure. But fuck it I'm going to wear it anyway, because I know what it means to me.

* * *

My daily run is simply 10 to 15 minutes out into the fields near where I live. Just enough to get my middle-aged heart beating, the blood pumping and a brief pause for the body on the hill top. There I can take in the beauty of the countryside and breathe in a few gulps of fresh air before running home.

This morning it was raining. How fabulous. To run in the rain is to feel the four elements at once. The firm earth under the feet, the rich air in the lungs, the warm fire of the heart, and the gentle water that so generously pours down from above, like nature's magic.

Today when I stopped on the hill top I was struck by something profound. It was as if I momentarily became the archetypal divine child of mythology. There I stood, rain from the heavens gracing my head and shoulders, and the rich soil of the earth supporting me. I was consciously sandwiched between heaven and earth, divine father and divine mother, and I was the divine child (as we ALL are).

Out there, in nature's cathedral everything becomes one. My struggles of the last four years become insignificant. There I feel blessed beyond measure and deeply alive. I experience the paradox of being a child of heaven and thus worth more than a million dollars and yet also strangely insignificant, for everything I see and touch has been there, and will be there, infinitely longer than me.

* * *

And my walking between two worlds (the Christian and the Druidic) loses any confusion in that place too. I can sense the power of the Celtic myths of the Mabon and of the powerful forces of nature that we anthropomorphise into gods and goddesses. And I can touch the hand of the Christ child there too, for he is representative of us all, of our own divine status as daughters and sons of God.

A powerful and beautiful experience to take, now, into my garden chapel.

* * *

I have been welcomed back to my old church The Priory to their annual Children's holiday club to speak to the kids about baptism and do a little magic. I had three groups of them all up at the main altar where the font is. At one point I got to talk to the whole of them at once and I asked them how many of them had been christened, by me. Lots of little hands shot up. Very touching.

* * *

I've been invited to perform my Soulful Magic at a huge Emerging Christianity Convention lead by my long term mentor Fr. Richard Rohr at Swanwick, in Derby. I can't wait to be able to share what I do with these open-minded Christians.

* * *

To meet Fr. Richard again, after so many years, was truly wonderful. He hugged me tightly and I knew I was supposed to be there. I felt as if the convention was going to be something of a watershed/a turning point for me.

Fr. Richard presented a session on Emerging Christianity and came out with such classic phrases as, "EC is an attempt at a whole new and different kind of Reformation," and "people are tired of being anti-anything," and "when you lose the mystical level you always overdo the moralistic."

He also spoke lovingly about his own spiritual father, St. Francis of Assisi, saying that St. Francis attacked the bishop of Assisi in this way. He went outside the walls of the city and did the job better. That's how he rebelled. He didn't waste his time fighting or being aggressive or defensive. He simply did his own thing, and did it better. I thought this was a super model for my own "Hedge-ministry."

Francis also did everything in his power to get his people to stay at the bottom or at the edge and never at the top. He didn't even want his friars to be priests/clergy. He said, "You can't preach the gospel if you're part of the structures of power. You can't critique the system if you're a beneficiary of it." What powerful words!

* * *

I'm in awe. Last night I performed my show to my mentor and his people, as well as over 400 Emerging Christians from various denominations (the majority Roman Catholic). I decided to tell my whole story, warts and all. Afterwards so many people came and shared their support, warmth and encouragement. It moved me to tears. In fact two ladies came up and said, "we just want to embrace you, and do what the church should have done when you originally had the courage to share your story to those with power over you." And they just hugged me tightly, for some time. It was healing and beautiful.

* * *

I've just attended another talk by Fr. Richard, what Emerging Christianity is not! He said that EC is not oppositional and is non-dualistic, and also that Jesus, with sayings like "let the wheat and the weeds grow together" and "my Father's love shines on the good and the bad," was the first non-dualistic teacher of the West. "Jesus was far happier for us to live with the shadow rather than to project it" said Rohr. He also reminded us that all religious language is metaphorical; that there is no other language available. Non-dualistic metaphorical language was Jesus' way; it was his technique for teaching. He said things such as, "The kingdom of heaven is *like* ..." In other words he was open and honest about his use of metaphor. Rohr said that dualistic thinking is necessary for us to live/survive, but there comes a point where it can go no further, it hits the ceiling, especially when it comes to describing spirituality or God.

Other classic Rohr statements I picked up were:

"The ego always says 'no;' it hates change and cannot cope with discomfort. The soul always says 'yes.' Yes to what is. It is the inner trusting and un-defended vulnerable Self."

"Faith clearly means 'to move forward without knowing.' But for the last 300 years at least it's meant 'to know every-thing with certainty.' How has a word come to mean the exact opposite of what is originally meant?"

Later on in the bar Fr. Richard came up to me and, with a hug, said, "Your magic performance last night! How do you do that Mark? You say you're not psychic but I think you must be."

* * *

I've just finished reading *Jesus for the Non-Religious* by Bishop Jack Spong. It's a totally remarkable book. The scholarship is thorough, leaving no stone unturned. And what do we end up with? A fully human Jesus who broke down the tribal barriers and boundaries that separated people from people. He (Jesus) was real, a real human being, who lived, preached, threatened the religio-political establishments and was killed by them as a result. He pointed to that deep, servant like and self-assured human spirit which was so in touch with whom he was that he was willing to not cling on to it. His was a fully surrendered life. This human portrait of Jesus is perhaps a little like a first century Jewish equivalent of the Buddha around whom massive mythic/non literal stories have been encased.

For Spong, Jesus points us to the God (non-theistic "isness"/the ground of being) who exists in all. He is thus not God, yet is God in the sense that we all are. The difference with Jesus is that he had come to live more completely from that knowledge. Surely this Jesus is far more in common with modern day Neo-Paganism than modern day Christianity.

Maybe that deep truth of our own God-ness and therefore our brother/sisterness (and deep connectedness to all things) is what all "spiritually in tune" people really teach?

The following passage from the Wiccan *Charge of the Goddess* (in mythic language) seems to suggest something quite similar:

And therefore let there be beauty and strength, power and compassion, honour and humility, mirth and reverence within you. And thou who thinkest to seek Her, know thy seeking and yearning shall avail thee not unless thou knowest the mystery; that if that which thou seekest thou findest not within thee, then thou wilt never find it without thee.

September

I've just arrived at Canterbury for the second time this year. The hotel at the Cathedral is amazing. This is where I'll be staying. Luxurious.

I'm here for a huge weekend event called *The Gathering* which will host various speakers, performers and events including a live debate between Archbishop Rowan Williams and satirical Comedian/Private Eye Editor Ian Hislop. I wonder what this weekend has in store for me.

* * *

My goodness what a picture to wake up to, the Mother church of my own tradition. There she stands, proud and grandiose, just outside the hotel room window. I feel as if I'm a character in a Susan Howatch novel, though Salisbury would be the cathedral there (which she called Starbridge in her books).

* * *

I've just had breakfast with Ronald, the chap (a priest) who booked me for this event. It was really nice talking to him. He understood! He also lamented the current watering down of the Church of England's gift of inclusivity. Apparently, last night, when Archbishop Rowan had been in public debate in the cathedral, Ian Hislop had said something about how the Church of England is the kind of church that takes anyone and everyone; all those who have nowhere else to go. If only that were still true!

* * *

It's just been confirmed that a "round robin" email from someone based at my own Diocesan Office was indeed sent out to warn people about me. It has so blackened my name that it caused me to be questioned and very nearly cancelled from this very Canterbury based event. This almost certainly means that other Dioceses will, in some way or other, have had the note. Bang goes my ministry yet again. They're not going to touch me with a 50 foot barge pole now. Dammit. My God, haven't I suffered enough already? When's this going to stop? Alas, I still refuse to act in the same way. I will not stoop to their level over this. Those who did it can be confident at least that I will not publicise their names. They're lucky they were doing this to me and not someone else. What a mess though, and how on earth do I begin to counteract what they've done? In all truth I probably can't. It's most likely too late. The damage has been done.

* * *

I'm now in Devon and Cornwall for a few days of writing, studying and trips to various famous Pagan locations for research. I've also just taken part in my first ever Unitarian Church service. It's funny that the second bible reading was about ravens, the ones who fed the prophet Elijah. Ravens are messengers of God in that story. The Unitarians are lovely people. Their literature is very attractive. Very *me*.

* * *

These last few days have been so confusing. Canterbury was such a wonderful experience, and I have come away with a whole pile of excellent endorsements and recommendations, but I'm so sad and hurt after hearing about that email that was sent about me. After all the effort I put into contacting every single Diocese in the country! Canterbury might well have cancelled, were it not for my absolute assurance that I was no threat to the guy who booked me. It I had have been cancelled I'd have only made about £300 for the *whole* of September. As it happens I've not had any church bookings, or even any enquiries, for a few months now. Why do they hate me so much? Do they realise how punishing this is to me and my family? I've not hit back or kicked up a fuss. I've actually protected some of those who have been harshest towards me, yet now someone's trying to mess up even my Christian Magician work (which is something I had the *support* of my bishop to do).

* * *

I'm back in my favourite spot, The Reading Chair at Queenswood. This is the very forest that acts as a location for my novel *The Wizard's Gift*. Something drew me here this morning. I was on my way into Hereford to attend All Saints, but I simply had to drive into the forest car park and sit here to think and pray. I guess the Druid in me needed expressing today, rather than the Christian. I wonder if she'll show up, my raven soul-friend? Weird. I feel safe here, at peace, held, wrapped in a blanket of magic. Mmm that's nice. The cup of cafe latte I picked up from the car park café tastes good.

It's Sunday. I felt the need, the pull, to go to church and yet I ended up here in this enchanted spot. This is the imaginary place where my character Sam Harper (*The Wizard's Gift*) took a walk into the thick, dense, wood and ended up at a Druidic clearing. I feel like I'm there now.

Great Spirit; Spirit of this place, this sacred grove, speak to me. What do you have to say?

* * *

It was later than it should have been but I have just managed to celebrate Lammas (early harvest) outside in my back garden, with an apple offering.

How wonderful. I'm sitting outside with the warm late summer sunlight shining down and the wind blowing gently across my face. Signs of growth and harvest fruit are all around. Berries hanging heavy on branches and leaves beginning their gradual colour transformation. How awesome to be fully plugged into the magic of nature.

* * *

I've just received an invitation from someone who's seen me perform: it's to attend an evangelism convention and lead some presentations. She actually asked me if I was a Christian, which made me feel really good. She had already offered the invitation, so (presumably) even if I was not a Christian, I would still have been welcome to perform for them. How refreshing.

I must confess that I still love attending Christian and church-based conventions and events. I feel I have so much left to offer them. I still get excited about what I take and share. I am so sad about the email that was sent out to try to stop churches booking me. I still don't know how to play that one, but at least it has not (yet) filtered down to the person who booked me for the evangelism convention.

* * *

Today I attended the Cornovii Grove autumn equinox, and it was wonderful to be there again. The venue was the amazing Whitlenge near Kidderminster, a Druid themed landscape garden centre, open to the public, and run by the delightful Keith and Fran Southall. The ritual was in their meadow and I was invited to give peace to the quarters which felt so good. It was a powerful ceremony. I found the casting of the circle (where we create ritual or sacred space by symbolically drawing a circle around the group) especially moving and emotional today. I'm not really sure why but I just felt held by the great cosmic circle of magic. The grove members' beautifully spontaneous offering of various kinds of fruit and poetry was electrifying. After it was over, we all tasted the fruit. Gorgeous!

* * *

So when is it going to end? Now a bishop from a different Diocese, and one who was originally happy to endorse my magical ministry has pulled out! Why? Because he'd "heard something about me" (say no more). Meanwhile all my *real* friends keep saying, *"Fuck them all Mark, they're such a bunch of self-serving hypocrites."* But I can't. I still love the Church of England.

* * *

I really should get used to this but synchronicity still habitually awakens me to the magic all around. I'm just about to do a job down in Sussex. So I thought I'd pop in and see my cousin (whom I have not seen in years) and she offered me a bed for the night. I punched the postcode into Google maps and, wow, she lives in the next avenue to the Chief Druid Philip Carr-Gomm. I'll have to call by and see him while I'm there.

* * *

I'm driving to London to be interviewed for another possible TV documentary, but am presently stuck on the M4 at Junction 6. The last thing I heard was 40 minutes' delay. I hope this doesn't mean I miss the appointment. No movement whatsoever.

* * *

Wow, I just met Caroline from the TV company (whose office proudly displays their 8 BAFTAs). It turned out that she very much likes the idea of a documentary on Magic and Christianity with me presenting something as priest who is also a magician. Exciting.

* * *

I've just visited my cousin Ruth in Lewes before driving on to do some magic for a posh boarding school in Sussex. I've also just had a phone call from home. We're totally out of food and money and we're going to have to loan some. What is this all about? What are we going to do? Something's got to happen. We simply can't go on like this. I prayed to God for an answer: Father, Great Spirit, Wizard of all, unseen force, loving parent, what course of action should I take now? What do I? What do I do with my life? It feels so desperate. What do I do to hold it all together?

(And my inner voice said)

Mark, little brother, look around you.

Be at peace.

You're in your cousin's home.

Look. Look at the photos of the little "second cousins" of yours.

They've been in this world all this time and now is the first time you've actually seen them.

Life runs at such a fast pace.

It's all so quick and pressurised that you miss what you have little brother.

Be at peace and realise that everything has its place,

even the things you find hard, confusing, even terrifying are able to help you through your process of transformation.

Everything you struggle with is a potential lesson for growth.

Come back to me Mark my little brother.

And trust.

I will. But who are you?

I am the Source,

the deepest part of your soul.

My voice is but a whisper,

so I can be hard to hear when other voices shout and demand.

Are you God?

I am.

I am the God/dess voice within you and all people.

I am the "you" that you know exists,

yet all your striving for success and perfection makes it impossible to become.

Come back to me Mark.

I am always here.

I am the still, small voice.

Your current spiritual search is good but it is also cluttering your soul.

You don't need to feel so disconnected, disjointed, uprooted.

ALL your experiences are valid,

but whenever any one of them begins to dominate in a literal way it robs you of your peace and rootedness.

The Christian,

The Druid,

The Buddhist,

The Wiccan,

The Taoist,

The Jungian,

The Magical are all part of the story,

but none of them are the WHOLE story.

Just allow yourself to be carried by the Source which is known deeply inside you.

It is ME Mark.

All the forms, ideas, myths, deities, pictures of the divine are there to help plug you back into the God-in-you,

NOT to focus on the externals.

You will NOT find me "out there."

You will only ever find me inside your very depths; your deepest core of being is ME.

* * *

I paid a visit to the enormous chalk man called The Long Man of Wilmington which is inscribed on the side of a hill. Then I travelled on to St. Bede's school which was great. The teacher, a Mr. Waring, was fantastic and I was delighted to be able to offer some good magical advice for their school production of Peter Pan. He wanted to know how to levitate five children at once convincingly. He was delighted with my suggestions, especially after having thought that it would take a lot of money and a lot of apparatus to produce the effect. I showed him how he could do it for just a few quid. And then who did I bump into at the school but Philip's wife, Stephanie Carr-Gomm. How marvellous.

* * *

It happens all the time. I get so stressed up and upset by the church, but then I find myself coming back to it again and again. And there are two things that draw me back, two highly connected things. The first is Jesus himself. I have moved so far in my understanding of him, yet I seem to love him more deeply now than ever before. His beautiful human compassion moves me so much. I can see him as a man who was so transparent to God's love and grace that no wonder people saw him as divine. Indeed in this sense he is divine, he is son of God, moving us to look within and recognise our own son and daughter of God status. The second thing that draws me back to the church is when I come across church people who also reflect that divine Christ-like compassion. *And there are many.*

* * *

I've just been invited to speak about my open funeral liturgies at All Saints Church, Hereford. They're putting on a series throughout late autumn where speakers from different perspectives share insights around the theme of death and dying. One of them will be Bishop John Shelby Spong. How exciting to know that I'll be able to meet him at last. He's been a mentor since my days at theological college.

* * *

Ok I'm beginning to think that I am coming under fire from some sort of "psychic attack." A few years ago (when I was a "clever" liberal priest) I would have never imagined myself saying or even thinking such a thing. But now I do feel that energy can be used in this way; bad energy (or maybe "negative energy" is a better term)! Where it's coming from I do not know, though I could be forgiven for thinking "Christians." After all, I've seen many Christians involve themselves in black magic over the years. They wouldn't call it that of course. No, to them its "intercessory prayer" and they are "prayer warriors." But those on the receiving end (people who need "saving" from the "evil" they're involved in) don't view it as kindly prayer at all. It's more like being attacked by a psychic vampire. They feel drained and sapped of energy by those who continually send them their messages of so-called *prayerful concern*. I have a Wiccan friend who had to come off Facebook (and other online forums) to hide, after he was subjected to this form of "prayer" from his former friends (all born again Christians worrying for the state of his soul).

Today I need to begin learning how to deal with this and protect myself. I must also ask for the help of God/dess.

* * *

Well, a good seven months after my timing mistake (which brought me here over twelve hours early) I'm back at Sheffield University. It was a very easy trip on the road with my new satnav. It took just under three hours from my home in Leominster to the Octagon where I'll be performing. I'm parked in the very same space as last time! Oh the memories. That long thirteen hour wait before performing, but also the amazing experience at the cathedral. *He* spoke to me back then. He said, *"I still have work for you!"* Since then I've wanted to run away from the church many times, but I've resisted. I still feel I have a place, even as someone at the edge.

And now I have this amazing contract for a new book called *Jesus through Pagan Eyes;* an opportunity, perhaps, to consolidate all my Christian and Pagan experiences. On that note I'll be back up here again in a few weeks to meet High priest Steven Critchley and Patricia Crowther, one of the founders of Wicca, Gerald Gardner's original High priestesses. The journey is astonishing. I feel battered and bruised, yet also alive to something quite incredible. There is a Spirit leading me, guiding me, taking me step by step into and through this Narnian Wardrobe, and out into a fully enchanted universe of magic and synchronicity.

* * *

I'm now sitting with an ice cold half pint of lager at a University Freshers' Ball, (with a James Bond theme). There's an *Odd Job* lookalike here and all sorts of Bond memorabilia, casinos and huge video screens playing 007 movies. It reminds me of last May, at Marcus Katz's home in the Lakes, when I held in my hand an actual tarot card from the film *Live and Let Die*. Doing magic for these kids is a beautiful experience. I love it. I love bringing wonder and astonishment to them, and seeing the pleasure light up their faces.

* * *

Today's local paper *The Hereford Times* has a front cover story about Graham Hellier, an ex-school teacher of mine, about his "blasphemous" new book *Free-range Christianity*. It's been banned from the local Christian bookshop. He questions the virgin birth (yawn), the divinity of Jesus and other old chestnuts. More please. Let's get these "heretical" books out there. Let's make people think, after all most of it's such old hat.

* * *

I'm sitting watching all these delightful young people of Sheffield University come into the Ballroom for their Freshers' Night. It's quite an amazing experience. I am so aware of the uniqueness of every one of them. How immensely valuable they are, like little walking divine lights, each of them gifted in a unique way. I wonder what their families are doing right now. Their parents! Are they thinking about their children? I am thinking of mine. My two "divine lights" went back to their mum's again tonight. I love them so much. I miss them tremendously. The new way we do things means that they're now at their mum's for two weeks at a time. I miss them both *constantly*.

* * *

I'm back home and in awe of my time in Sheffield. While I was there I went to meet and stay with my old friend Steve again. I hadn't seen him in about twenty-five years. He and his partner Ed were so lovely to be with. They run a Wiccan Coven and I met some of the members too. It was my first ever time inside a Wiccan Temple. Breath-taking. Steve taught me so much. He also gave me the "Dryghtyn Prayer," a prayer that makes so much sense with regard to the whole polytheism vs. monotheism argument.

In the name of Dryghtyn, the Ancient Providence, who was from the beginning and is for eternity, male and female, the Original Source of all things; all-knowing, all-pervading, all-powerful; changeless, eternal.

In the name of the Lady of the Moon, and the Lord of Death and Resurrection.

In the name of the Mighty Ones of the Four Quarters, the Kings of the Elements.

Blessed be this place, and this time, and they who are now with us.

Taken from Witch Blood! The Diary of a Witch High Priestess! by Patricia Crowther, chapter four (1974, House Of Collectibles, Inc.).

* * *

I'm back in Sheffield again. Steve has just taken me to meet the "Grandmother of Wicca" Patricia Crowther (to whom the Dryghtyn Prayer is attributed). What a fascinating lady. It was so lovely to talk to and learn from her. She's also a puppeteer and (with her late husband) also used to perform magic (my kind of magic). She was delighted to learn that I was a magician and showed me a TV clip of when she appeared on a game show as a puppeteer. She wouldn't let me go without filling my pocket with a pile of chocolate biscuits for the journey.

* * *

I chatted to another Wiccan coven leader on the phone tonight, my friend Scott. He said I should wake up to the fact that my family (the church) have actually ceased being my family now. And that I should cut my losses and go a different way. And as if to confirm what Scott said to me I've now seen the letter (round robin email) that was sent out to every other Diocese about me. Someone from Canterbury Diocese finally forwarded it to me to look at. It talks about me "not being licensed." But I hadn't claimed to be licensed because I wasn't offering myself as a priest. I was offering myself as a Christian Magician, and even my ex-bishop was in support of that. It's made it impossible for me now.

However what with all the trauma and anguish brought back by seeing the letter, an angel (out of the blue) has also emailed me. Philip Carr-Gomm sent a lovely note with some wise counsel: "Think of the bigger picture now Mark. Ask yourself what you *want* to be doing." Well, maybe the church *is* wrong for me now? Maybe it's time to call it a day and abandon Christianity like it has abandoned me?

* * *

I'm suddenly getting so much support from all over the planet, *literally*. And it's seriously influencing me. I'm being counselled, from every possible area, to make a decision to be even more daring and step into a consciously and public Paganism. *And thus to reject Christianity.*

On the other hand there is still the inner voice, which whispers away inside a corner of my mind: *Mark, you don't have to let them take away what has always been yours. You still have much work to do within the Christian scene.* I have even had a very supportive letter from my local MP saying that he'll come and see my bishop with me.

October

It's early October. The season has turned and the darker months are about to embrace us. The despair caused by that name blackening letter has taken me into an equally dark and menacing void. But the postal courier has just delivered something special, something that jolted my sense of purpose and reminded me what it is I'm about, the delivery of my new book *The Path of the Blue Raven*.

* * *

I'm now walking over the fields. Its dawn and I can see the glorious early morning moon above. She's still awake, smiling down from her place in the dark sky. And there, in the distance, the faint at first but gradually loudening and all too familiar voice of the croaking raven. Amazingly she flies right across the face of the moon. How enchanting!

And now I'm home again, and yet I can still hear her voice. She's even closer. I can still see the moon too. I look up and the blue black silky goddess sails in front of the moon for a second time. She's right over my home now; how magical, how awe-inspiring, how comforting.

* * *

I can't believe it. I'm here again. I'm at the Ammerdown Centre in Somerset and about to perform to all the high flyer clergy of the nation's *Greater Churches Group*. This is the place where, about ten years ago, I met three people who've been so important in my life over the last decade, Richard Rohr, Gerry Proctor and James Fahey, all three of them Roman Catholic. Fr. Richard has been a mentor figure ever since my one time spiritual director introduced me to his recorded sermons about fifteen years ago. The tape recording I listened to first was entitled *The Spirituality of Imperfection* and it was a real life changer.

When I met Rohr at Ammerdown in the year 2000 I'd already been listening to him for about five years. I'd been signed off work due to stress and was feeling pretty beaten up by life. My mentor sat next to me during the first meal and consequently offered me some personal private time which was such a blessing. I remember trying to articulate myself to him and getting all self-critical and apologetic. And then his words somehow enabled me to relax, like I hadn't in months, and to unwind into a deep feeling of acceptance and divine love. He was the first person to point out that I might be an Enneagram 4. Up until that point I'd been convinced of my status as an "unredeemed 1" (a terrible perfectionist). We talked about "personality types" and Rohr, master of the Enneagram and number 1 himself, simply smiled and said, *"Mark, I just don't see you as a 1. You're too gentle and non-judgemental. Why don't you check out 4s? Often 4s get muddled up with 1s."*

I also met Catholic priest Gerry Proctor and retreat house owner James Fahey, and have remained close friends with them both ever since. One not so pleasant memory (which involves these two guys) is of the final night when a gang of us decided to trek out into the forest, build a fire and tell stories. During the evening I didn't realise that someone was spiking my drinks. I had to be carried home through the mud and trees before spending the night throwing up, Gerry and James taking turns to watch over me. In the morning I woke to the most disgusting mess of mud, leaves and vomit all over the bed sheets.

However the most embarrassing moment was when I finally left the retreat house (which happened to be a convent) and said to the two sisters at the door, *"I'm so sorry sisters, but last night I soiled my sheets."* Their look of absolute horror suddenly made me realise how my badly worded phrase had been understood.

Any attempt at an explanation would have dug a deeper hole so I fled.

* * *

I've just heard from my local MP (a great guy who's been so supportive to me over the years). He's going to take me to see my ex-bishop next month. I told him I don't want my job back. I just want people to stop trying to ruin my life!

Unbelievably I just felt I needed to pull a tarot card. 78 shuffled cards. I just *knew* which one I'd pick, one of the 22 majors. Yes, that's what I expected, JUSTICE!

* * *

So what's tonight going to be like, performing for the clergy and people of *The Greater Church's Group*? I have to say that one of the many angels of the Church of England, a man from my own Diocese, is the Dean of Hereford Cathedral who is also chair of the Greater Church's Group. It was he who got me this booking. But are they going to like my stuff? Are they going to warm to me? Will this (perhaps) help me to get back out there onto the fringes of the C of E?

* * *

Oh wow. I feel so tearful and so very blessed. Last night was truly amazing, performing for the Greater Church's people. They were fantastic. I felt so appreciated, held and cared for. They were kind and supportive and genuinely helpful. And it gets better. I held the chalice this morning. These lovely people invited me to take the cup of the Eucharist within the beautiful morning service in the chapel. It was an honour and a joy. I am truly beginning to feel that I am a man of "dual-faith" honestly and truly. I also feel like I've made a mistake *(perhaps a big one)* in using obscure language to try to explain who/what I am, which has only ended up offending people and thus shooting myself in the foot.

* * *

I'm now at another gig and this one couldn't be more different from the last. I'm speaker/performer for a whole group of Rochester Diocesan Evangelists.

I came to this event with much trepidation but I've been met by a wave of warmth and love. It's being held at a Roman Catholic convent near London, with a simply gorgeous chapel. I've just listened to how utterly worn out and broken these sweet people are. And I've been impressed by their desire, not to force people into faith but to simply share their love of Jesus with others. I've decided to present the first part of my book *The Gospel of Falling Down*, which will enable me to speak to this theme of allowing ourselves to own the cracks, the flaws, the imperfections and dents which open us (not close us) to God's love.

Again this is confirmation that I still have a role in the Christian world, even if only to enable people to find and receive grace. Jesus' stories still send shivers down my spine by their power to reconnect us to the divine love in each of us.

I've been made to feel so very welcome here, in a quite surprising way. These people represent the other end of the spectrum as far as churchmanship and theology goes, yet they have blessed me with their humility, friendship and openness. I've even been asked to address them within the Sunday morning service's sermon slot. I'm going to have to be very honest with them and tell them that I still love and believe in Jesus but have a real problem with believing in the church.

* * *

I'm still with the Evangelists and I've just led a session which turned out to be a most beautiful experience. I didn't hold back at all, and shared my falling down material with a whole lot of honesty about me and my relationship with the church. And afterwards person after person came up to me sharing stories of pain and rejection (much of it self-rejection). I was ministering to these evangelical missionaries, *amazing!* I talked about the "mark of God" being in all people and that (in my opinion) evangelism is not so much about taking something to someone a (*as*) something that they do not already have but awakening them to the God (Christ) within them.

Then came my performance; my magic show. I cannot remember a presentation to a church group that has gone as well as this. They were lovely and so open to everything I did. In fact I could say they were eating out of my hands. It was also astonishing how many genuine synchronicities occurred during that performance. For example I did an effect which involved the playing card the 4 of Spades, and I said a little about how playing cards can be seen as archetypal. To demonstrate I used a Spanish deck of cards and showed them how the Spanish suits can relate to the Jungian personality types of the Myers Briggs system. I said the that 4 of Spades would be the Spanish 4 of Swords (I thought it would be going too far to also tell them that tarot suits were the same as Spanish playing card suits). However after I'd done this effect with a man named Phillipe, he stood up and told everyone that earlier that day he'd drawn a picture of a man with the 4 playing cards' suits around him.

Another example of how wonderful this event was becoming involves Caroline whom I spoke to originally when she booked me. She came up to me and told me of her huge appreciation of who she calls "The Tree People" (i.e. Pagans). It is becoming a truly extraordinary weekend.

* * *

I'm sitting here in the convent, looking out at the green surrounding fields. It seems, at last, with all the turmoil of my own rocky relationship to my local Diocese, I am now settling within a peaceful place of balance between two traditions. I really do not have to choose one over the other. I have said too much in the past; too much that has alienated my former life. In many ways I've been driven to it *but* I must not allow the minority of fear filled people to rob me of the whole picture. I still love the Christ, the symbolic god-man who was (in Jesus) a real historical figure. I love him but find his church too difficult. Yet I have found, even among these Diocesan Evangelists, a level of openness and warmth (even openness to my hurting, broken and Pagan side) that has taken me by delightful surprise.

Each moment here is becoming more and more blessed and enriched. A woman just shared a very painful story of her own life. It was very beautiful to see that the group (and leader) held her and supported her. She also talked about the little prophesying groups where people gather together and (when moved to do so) speak out "words of wisdom." Then people speak out what they feel moved to say. They can tell of visions, pictures, mythical/symbolic sayings. It all sounds so much more sensible and realistic than the tongue interpretations of my earlier Pentecostal experience. They seem to be opening themselves to their inner wisdom and natural magic.

Jackie Frost, well known Christian Leader Rob Frost's widow, is also having a major input in this weekend. She's now talking up front about her husband's death. She's energetic, inspirational, dynamic and (most importantly) *totally* vulnerable. She's talking about living with the mess, muddle and brokenness of his loss. Another thing that's so clear to me (among these evangelicals) is that prayer is magic. The amount of time I've heard them talking about prayer to change actual reality! These people really are very inspiring.

She's now talking about looking out for signs (synchronicities), and to notice the patterns that a benevolent force (God) is holding/directing.

Four points of Jackie's wisdom that spoke especially to me:

Be prepared to share the dark parts of your life.

Seek out people with whom you can be totally honest.

Pain becomes less powerful once you can do this.

Try not to think in terms of unbelievers/outsiders etc.

We're now involved in an imaginative/reflective exercise. We've been asked to listen to a John Denver song:

Sweet, sweet surrender,
Live, live without a care,
Like a fish in the water,
Like a bird in the air.

She closed her session with a beautiful open prayer; a prayer expressing (on behalf of us all) our letting go of ALL in our lives that holds us back.

After the session the leader, Jean, took me to one side and said, *"Mark, there's something about you as a person, that has enriched us. Perhaps you're not aware of that?"* Again I'm being affirmed and valued here in a way I never imagined.

* * *

I've just spent a few moments in the beautiful convent chapel again. I walked over to the smaller chapel with the tabernacle, and genuflected. It felt natural and right to do so, *and then I wept.*

There's absolutely no doubt that I still feel deeply connected to Christ, to the Christ in me and in others. And these people, these revved up/loved up evangelists, have without doubt shared His love with me over these few days. Christ is alive to them, clearly.

And He has been re-awakened (once again) within me too. I feel as though they have indeed been evangelists to me! Not in the usual manner of introducing me to something I did not possess, but in the sense of awakening me to something beautiful within. They enabled me to awaken the sleeping Christ inside my heart.

I now feel more grounded and more whole. I still feel the same towards the church, but the Christ is alive again. He, the man, the human Jesus, was so awakened to his inner Christ-ness that he was able to connect others to theirs, and he still does so. *This is evangelism.*

There is only Oneness, Spirit, experienced the world over in many and various ways, by many and various cultures and religions. All point to the same source. I have become truly eclectic.

* * *

Oh my word, this gets even more extraordinary by the minute. I've just been part of a breath-taking communion service. I preached but I did not preach. I simply felt moved to share my *whole* story to the evangelists, and then read my piece *The Tale of the Two Lost Sons* from one of my books. I pulled no punches and gave them the whole deal. I allowed myself to become naked and totally vulnerable within this evangelical circle. At the end the leader, Jean, with tears in her eyes, came over to me and said, "I feel called to tell you this," and she took off her coloured silk scarf and hung it round my neck. She then said, "I wish I had a stole to give you but this will do. Mark never forget that you are a priest, and *never* let anyone take that away from you. Keep this scarf as a reminder." [It's been on my altar to this day]. I was knocked over by it, totally. These people have awakened me to my Christian priesthood again. Thanks be to God. I have a new direction now, not to go one way or the other but I know that I most definitely still have a role to play in the Christian world.

After that I was just smothered in love and hugged tightly by just about everyone there. I also had an apology. A woman came up to me and offered *"an apology from the Body of Christ. God weeps for you,"* she said, *"and for how his church has caused you such pain."* Then, a little later, at the dinner table, a whole pile of these delightful evangelists said in unison, *"We've reinstated you as a priest. You don't need the church to appoint you. You're a priest in the order of Melchizedek."* Unforgettable!

* * *

I'm now driving home from a meeting with my brother in magic, Rob Chapman, and had to stop. Rob lives in Oswestry over a second hand book shop. He took me down into the shop to see some interesting old first editions. I held an original copy of John Barrie's Peter Pan, worth about £1,000 or more. Also I had a flick through an original copy of Gerald Gardener's Witchcraft Today (again first edition) worth £200. Amazing.

But I had to stop because of something that has just occurred to me about the recent evangelists' convention and the genuine synchronicities that I witnessed during my magic act there. Why did it happen? Why did it flow so smoothly, in an environment that I supposed would be harder to perform within, not easier?

Two reasons I think:

1) I had thoroughly prepared myself. All week before I'd been using various spiritual exercises so I was open.

And 2) (and most importantly) the people themselves were open. They were open because they were broken, vulnerable, expectant, believing and *at the edge*.

They are an undervalued, misunderstood, and at the edge ministry within the church. Whether you happen to value their ministry or not you can't deny that (within the Church of England) they are not seen as mainstream *and they feel it*. They were vulnerable before I even arrived. Of course sometimes vulnerable people can go into defence mode and become completely impregnable, but other times they can just symbolically collapse and let go of all resistance, let down their defences. This is what happened I believe. They trusted each other, trusted their leader, trusted the other speakers and trusted me. And, being the type of Christians who expect Spirit to move, bingo, *magic* and lots of it. It was a demonstration of *The Gospel of Falling Down* occurring right before my eyes. The cracks in these people became windows through which the light shone out, and some of it was so bright that it almost blinded me.

In contrast a Curates' convention/raining weekend in Swanwick (again largely evangelical, and far more male) I recently spoke at, was precisely the opposite. There the people were generally closed, suspicious, self-secure and (to be quite frank) arrogant. Thus my message was not listened to and no magic flowed what so ever. It was a struggle, a real struggle.

* * *

I've just been to Glasshampton Monastery, a Franciscan house near Great Whitley. This was my first visit in about eighteen years. I stayed there for my pre-theological college selection retreat back in the mid '90s. This time I met Revd. Peter Walley, chaplain to the Bishop of Litchfield (he'd seen me perform at their Diocesan Convention earlier in the year). He was so gentle and caring to talk to and really wanted to help me find some sense of peace. I told him my whole story and he listened without judgement, expressing (like the woman at the evangelists' convention) an apology for how the church had hurt me.

* * *

I just had a special moment with my mother the Goddess. I looked at my diary for the next two months. It's now October and this time of year (late autumn to winter) should be the busiest time of year. I should be able to rely on this Harvest/Christmas period to financially boost the quieter times of year. Yet I saw the two and a half months' worth of blank pages staring up at me from my open appointment calendar. By this time last year I had about ten bookings for winter by now. *Clearly I'm now being avoided* I thought to myself. I felt scared and hurt and knelt at my altar before the gentle smiling Goddess (Our Lady of Vladimir) and, after a while, she seemed to whisper something:

"Mark, do not fear. Trust. Continue to live with integrity. Don't sell out. Trust. All will be well. To be true, authentic, does cost ... enormously. But it also has unseen rewards in so many other areas. Trust, all will be well."

"Thank you my mother," I whispered in response.

* * *

This evening I heard Bishop John Shelby Spong speak live. What an incredible experience! Mind blowing, truly. What a man. The most beautiful thing was the deep love expressed to his wife Christine. It was so tangible, their deep connection. He even spoke of the love that is strangely expressed through nature as the wild honey bee fertilises etc.

His answer to the question from my friend, a priest called Marcus, was so telling. Marcus asked him how you can be a liberal/progressive priest (or bishop) in a conservative environment. Spong said he'd never served liberal churches. He was based in the South of the USA and always at conservative churches. His wisdom was to simply say, *"You just have to love them. The secret is to love all the people and lead from the front"* he said. *"Step out and give them space to catch up, in love."*

* * *

It's nearly Halloween and today I'm being taken round some Herefordshire and Worcestershire hospitals to do "tricks with treats" for the children on the wards. It's with Sunshine Radio, so the whole thing can be aired too. What a lovely idea. It turned out to be a very moving day with Hayley the presenter who drove me round the two counties.

* * *

Today is the 31st October and I'm on my way to a totally new experience for me. I've done the Druid thing for a while now. I've also been present at a very open and eclectic Glasgow Wiccan ceremony. I've spent time in a Sheffield based Wiccan temple. But I've never been to a closed coven Sabbat, and that's what I'm on the way to now, and it's Halloween/Samhain. I got onto the M25 (North West) and it seemed the moon was somehow strangely guiding/leading me. Then I got closer to the area of the temple, a long wide road, the moon hung there right at the end of the road. It was a haunting sight. And I arrived, a parking space right outside. Perfect.

It was an immense privilege for me to be part of this ceremony because normally only Alexandrians would be allowed. I'd been invited because the High Priest saw me as a fellow magical initiate, albeit of a different tradition (Druidry).

* * *

It's quite remarkable sitting here and watching the coven at work. They (we in fact) have spent two whole hours so far cleaning, polishing, preparing, tidying, cooking and setting up the temple for the ceremony/feast. It's quite amazing. They all work together with discipline and duty, each having their own special tasks to attend to. All serving their God and Goddess on this, their New Year's celebration. This night, Halloween as these people of the Craft prefer to call it, is their most holiest of nights.

[The contents of the night must remain a secret].

Huge excitement! After weeks of struggling with how to begin the new book project *Jesus through Pagan Eyes* I've just found the key.

I'm to use the most up to date and progressive Christian biblical scholarship to attempt to present a de-Christed Jesus, and then move on to a more mythic unpacking of what we mean by Christ. Both of these, the human Jesus and the mythic Christ, will then be set against and compared with modern Pagan under-standings of Jesus and Christ.

* * *

I've realised that I've become a "cyber-pastor" or "cyber-priest" or maybe even "cyber-counsellor." Many people now write to me for spiritual advice and guidance because of my retreats, books and performances. I find it an immense privilege but it can be very time consuming and often exhausting.

* * *

How exciting it is to find yourself on a new quest. A quest for meaning. A quest for answers. And so I have now begun my new book *Jesus through Pagan Eyes*, a quest if ever there was one. I have my direction.

- Recover (for Pagans) the historical Jewish Jesus using the scholarship of the Jesus Quest.
- Define the church's Jesus-Christ, as portrayed in many Gospel passages and embellished/highlighted with neon lights in the church's creeds.

- Recognise the mythic dimension to Jesus-Christ.
- Bring to light other Christ's i.e. the gnostic Christ of Thomas etc.
- Present a picture of the Cosmic/Universal Christ.

* * *

Things are looking up. All Saints Hereford was beautiful yesterday (Sunday Mass) and tomorrow is my talk there (in the Spong series). A London based vicar has also just invited me to her church to speak too. She does shamanic travel and tarot.

November

All Saints Church Hereford, *Doing Death Differently*. What an experience. I was invited to speak on the subject of death and dying, but from the perspective of a freelance eclectic minister. I told them about my journey into Druidry. There were many clergy there and there was only one difficult question to deal with. The whole experience blew my mind. All Saints was the first church that originally sponsored me for ordination. How perfect that this is now also the first time I've publicly lectured on my death and re-birth as a non-denominational priest.

* * *

It's now late November and it's Sunday. I'm with my sister at her church, *Challenge Community Church.* Though not my style of church it was lovely. There were lots of nature based psalm/hymns in praise of the oceans, sun and moon. And a video display to accompany the songs with photo images.

The speaker was from *Christians Against Poverty*, a very impressive organisation which my sister works for. They help struggling people get themselves out of financial difficulty. Brilliant. I'm very proud of my sister who's becoming the CAP Manager for Herefordshire.

I heard my raven again today. My beautiful magic companion who, every so often reminds me that magic is with me every step.

* * *

I've just had the meeting with my bishop and MP, and it was okay. I was so churned up. It had been two and a half years since he asked me to resign and I'd not seen him since then. He apologised for the horrible time I'd had and my MP was just great. The whole issue regarding the nasty email was brushed to one side, but the MP didn't seem concerned about that. He had higher plans. He clearly wanted to get me back into work as a full time priest, to be reinstated. I'd already said that I didn't want my job back but it seemed that it was actually an option now. The bishop said that it was indeed about time I started thinking about making my way back in now that the initial "problem" I came to him about had been dealt with. However he then brought up a new, secondary, problem that had developed around me since my resignation back in 2007, my flirtation with the Pagan world. His conclusion was that I would need to sit down with an appointed priest who would "test my orthodoxy." If I can come a little way under the umbrella of orthodoxy then I can come back in.

I got home and there was an answer phone message waiting for me. A woman was asking about retreats. I rang her back and (synchronicity) we chatted and got on brilliantly. We even had a "word of wisdom" for each other. She told me how she was "at the edge" herself and needs to find others who are in that place between places. If I were to come back under the umbrella of orthodoxy and become a regular vicar again I'd have a ministry in the church of course, but I'd be losing people like her. In fact I'd be robbing them of my own story, a story that could really speak to them. And, perhaps even more importantly, I'd be robbing myself of them. I don't think I can do it, I really don't think I can.

So at the end of this very Pagan drenched year I've now been offered a way back into the establishment and a life of security too. A home, pension, salary, ministry and respect in the community. But can I do it? I don't think I can. I think I have to remain true to self, God/dess, my brothers and sisters in the Pagan and Progressive Christian worlds.

The way of the hedge-priest does not pay in financial terms, but it's the only way for me now. To regain my vicar's job at that price (denying my Pagan side) would surely be to sell my very soul.

And then …

What a wonderful conversation I've just had with Philip Carr-Gomm. He actually advised me to go for it, to go through the "orthodoxy test." He said I should to be totally true to myself and actually "test" the Church of England, to see if *it* is big enough for *me*!

He'd be really interested in the results he said. Interesting. *Think think think.*

* * *

Just two days after meeting the bishop and receiving his invitation back into ministry within the Church of England and here I am on Advent Sunday, back where it all began, St.Laurence's Church Ludlow. It's for the final farewell of my one time Training Incumbent, Dr. Brian Curnew, Team Rector of the Ludlow Group. As I sit here at the back of the colossal church, trying to take in everything within the liturgy, I ask myself *in all integrity could I really be part of this (officially) again?* I get my pen out and make notes on the order of service, highlighting any of the more difficult phrases in the liturgy and creed. It's a particularly formal service, with a language and general tone that has never done anything for me, but this is the place where I began my ordained life and it's not easy to think of how far things have strayed since then.

And now tears fill my eyes because it's the moment in the service where we share the Peace with one another. Brian the Rector has worked his way right down to the back of the church to me. He said, "I've come down here because I saw you. I'm so glad you're here" and he gave me a huge hug. This faith stuff, this religion stuff, is not about words, or even beliefs, it's about relationships and people.

December

I'm at another church now, Bewdley Parish Church. The vicar, Keith, has been so good to me over the last couple of years. He's invited me back to speak and perform for a school Advent service. The children have all just been singing, and it brings a lump to my throat. I miss this so very much.

* * *

I've just been told that there's more gossip about me and one priest has been overheard objecting to me saying, "He's trying to have his cake and eat it." If I knew who this was I'd be inclined to write them a friendly note pointing out that having any kind of cake is well beyond my means at the moment, and that the phrase is actually almost the exact antithesis of my current status.

* * *

I'm at Tenbury Wells Mistletoe Blessing Ceremony. This is such a wonderful event. Every year the local Druid group comes here annually to process through the town carrying symbolic mistletoe, which Tenbury Wells is famous for, and then hold a huge public blessing ceremony near the river. I usually come wearing both clerical collar and Druidic cloak, to demonstrate that two faiths can live together within these beautiful nature based traditions. I find it powerful and deeply moving to stand within this huge circle made up of Druids, Christians and many members of the local community who just happened to be passersby.

* * *

I'm so fortunate to still have mentors and soul friends like Fr. Richard Rohr et al., Christian men and women who speak and share love in the name of Christ. There are many such people out there. However I'm really not sure if I can go back into the churchian world myself, so much of it does not ooze love and compassion but judgement and wrath. I actually feel that I am orthodox enough, in fact I know that I'm far more orthodox than many of the official clergy I rub shoulders with, but I don't think the church is Jesus-centred enough. It may indeed harm me spiritually to go back.

* * *

I've just been taken for a meal by a very well-known local solicitor and brethren lay-preacher. He looked me up because he'd heard about my Druid connections and wanted to hear some more about it, first-hand. We had a very warm and interesting discussion, and it turned out that he knew far more about modern Druidry and its customs than I expected an evangelical preacher to know. He also seemed to have a much more generous attitude towards it than I'd met even from certain fellow liberal Anglicans. We also talked about faith in general and I suddenly felt safe enough to share my entire story of failure, confession and consequent resignation with him. When I told him how it all ended up he glared, thumped the table with his fist and shouted. *"There's no scriptural justification for punishing a repentant sinner!"* Needless to say, I've never forgotten that, the day when even an ultra-conservative evangelical preacher objected to my treatment.

* * *

My God! I could have died, *literally*. I've just driven back from a late night magic gig in Milton Keynes. I was on a motorway and obviously didn't realise how tired I was. I fell asleep at the wheel. Terrifying. And stupid.

* * *

As a magician I am often asked to use magic within my ceremonies, sometimes even within funerals. I see the practice of stage Magic (illusion) as a tool which keeps alive the hope of real magic and is often a gateway for powerful synchronicities. Today I had the privilege of conducting a funeral ceremony for a man who had a passion for butterflies. He was a writer and had once written a novel about a butterfly. I also learned from his widow that, shortly after the heart attack which immobilised him, a great cloud of butterflies flew up and surrounded him. And, even on the day of his death a butterfly was spotted trying to get into his room. I must add that his widow had also told me that he loved magic. I put together a ceremony and used this butterfly image as a theme closing the ceremony with a symbolic and magical blessing. With the aid of a little "conjuring" I created the effect of a whole cloud of coloured paper butterflies, which flew up and scattered over his coffin. After the ceremony the family and I travelled to the crematorium and then returned to the house for the wake. When we arrived we were stunned for, there in the kitchen, dancing like fairies, were two red admirals, and it's December. Magic? Well whether it was or not it was most certainly magical.

* * *

I'm still not 100 per cent sure what to do with regard to my offer back into full time ministry and the orthodoxy test. God, who am I? And what is my calling now?

Mark, you ask who you are, but your question really ought to be "who are you not?"

When you ask who you're not you will gradually begin to release the layers, the barriers, and the obstacles to who you really are.

When you cling to what/who you think you are you will not remember who you truly are. The irony is that you DO know who you are, as does every creature on earth, but the human memory has been temporarily overshadowed by the ego. The ego is the part of your consciousness that thinks it's you, and you believe it. Beneath the voices, the ego/persona, lies the deep hidden gold of your true Self. There also is where you find Me. What you call "Christ," the Christ spark is that inner mark of God/dess which IS your true Self.

Jesus became Christ when he discovered this very truth. Countless others have also achieved this, but do not let the word achieve mislead you. Achieve should not imply a struggle or a striving. Struggle and strife merely add more layers to the false-self and thus creates more spiritual amnesia. The "way" is not to add but to subtract. The Buddha and the Christ found their true Selves by being able to live lightly to the "surface persona" and by letting go of everything the ego thought would make them who they were.

You and all sentient beings are also Christs/Buddhas, yet ones who've simply forgotten their true identity.

Therefore spend time considering what you are not and in so doing begin to remember what/who you are.

I think I know what I need to do. I will compose a grateful letter to the bishop, but decline. I will state that my priesthood remains intact and that I'm as far under the orthodox umbrella as I feel I need to be, but that I must remain free for the time being.

I've known Christ for over 20 years and it's been *real*. It has been the church that has robbed me (from time to time) of this mystical love. All my new discoveries and encounters/experiences have added to this essential "in-Christ-ness." I have actively tried to distance myself from church and even Christ from time to time, but he keeps pulling me back in. I have developed a Druidic heart but Christ still speaks (through the inner wizard) and I am still his priest. *There is no need to be in any conflict.*

Jesus is the man in whom the Christ was somehow strangely embodied. Others have also embodied this Christ-ness, not least the Buddha. Christ is the concept/reality of an incarnating spark of God in all things. This is a panentheistic approach to the divine.

* * *

I'm at Hereford Cathedral doing some magic for the boy choristers. What fun. I love being here and get a huge lump in my throat every time I am. Oh the memories; the warm feelings of being a Church of England cleric. Will it ever leave me? Will I ever get over the sense of loss? I met the teacher Matthew, who's a lovely guy and Canon Piper who always makes me smile, another great priest of the Diocese. I'm always able to be myself here. I so miss it.

* * *

The extraordinary novelist, Phil Rickman, invited me to be interviewed as a "vicar who hangs out with witches" at one of his 'meet the author' evenings in Leominster library. Nearly 100 people showed up. One thing that really struck me from what he said was with regard to the work of fantasy authors. He really does not like the fantasy genre, because he's irritated by the desire to create that which they don't already see here (i.e. in this world). He said that in his own explorations and research for the writing of novels he always finds the weird and the wonderful wherever he goes. There is always a magic, right here, right under our feet. We don't need to invent it. We just need to look.

* * *

I had a Jesus moment today. While researching for my book *Jesus through Pagan Eyes* I suddenly became powerfully aware that Jesus' followers did experience something dramatic and life-changing shortly after his death. It was probably not what the gospels portrayed as they looked back through the eyes of inter-pretation, but it was something of an experience that he was still very much with them.

I felt a similar presence as I sat and read. This has happened to me a few times over the last few years. Clearly I am a man of two paths, dual-faith, but what is heart-warming is that this teacher from Nazareth still moves me deeply and still has a powerful place in my life. He is a mirror to the God I experience in myself.

It's just occurred to me as I write this, that about an hour before that experience I was awestruck by the sun. It was snowing but the sun glared through the window and (as I explained in an email to someone in the USA) it purged my mind. I prayed to God as it happened. Christ is the divine energy (the sunlight of heaven) that was burning powerfully within the human Jesus and which is found glittering away in all people. Also it is what is seen/experienced in the Avatars of the spiritual. Amazing.

* * *

I've just received a contract from Llewellyn for the new book. Fantastic.

* * *

My daughter's had her GCSE exam results back. I don't know where she gets it from (Mark Townsend O Level Art). They are excellent. I need to go and buy her a gift to say congratulations. She'll be off to college now. Where does time go?

* * *

As I walked this morning I received an astonishing insight from a "sacrament" I was holding in my hand. I was making my way up a hill reading the spiritual masterpiece *You Are the Light* by Brother John Martin Sahajananda and making occasional notes on the pages as different things struck me. And after a while I noticed that the pen I'd been holding was missing. Well, part of the pen was missing. I was still holding onto the plastic shell of it, but the interior ink cartridge had fallen out. I suddenly had nothing to write with. And almost immediately a thought struck me. I could no longer write because my pen had become empty. This was the precise message that I'd just been reading from Brother John Martin about the kingdom of God. Stop, empty yourself (of self/ego) and you will find your true Self (the inner kingdom). Or stop trying to fill yourself with this "correct" doctrine, interpretation, religious observation and recognise that all such activity (mental, psychological, emotional, physical), and all our attempts to "earn" our way to the kingdom are, in fact, barriers not gateways. Our own inner and empty Self is the only gateway we need. So stop, empty yourself of all your striving, and know that you are already IN the kingdom of God and the kingdom of God is in you. That was what I saw as lesson 1 from my pen. Then came lesson 2.

I really did need to continue to take notes (if only to note what I'd just learned) so I decided to retrace my steps to see if I could remember the point where I'd lost the inside of my pen. And it hit it me - *POW!* For a while I have been confused (lost even). Certain thoughts, ideas, notions have brought peace, but others have brought immense unrest/disharmony within both my Druid and Christian experience. It struck me that once again my lost pen cartridge had provided a metaphor and an answer. The way to reconnect to the peace I have lost is not to try to solve it with the mind (there can be no real "peace of mind" because minds are obstacles to peace) and work it all out, but to travel back to the point where I'd lost sight of the peace. To revisit the last point when I knew I had peace, and then to journey forward again and notice where the un-peace crept in.

Usually (for me anyway) unrest/un-peace comes in when my tendency to literalise and make exclusive my beliefs rises to the surface. Or to add a thought/belief/practise that contradicts my inner gut experience. The key lesson here is that our heart knows what is wholesome, soulful, uplifting and healthy, and anything that robs this is not to be given the same level of acceptance. So for me I noticed that I began to lose some of my peace when I started to place myself inside a "box" which ruled out total exclusivity and unconditional divine love.

I now ask myself what is the core essence of my heart's faith, i.e. the simplest form of my beliefs which bring a sense of peace not unrest?

1 God – Spirit, Divine energy is everywhere and is in all things. Immanent and transcendent. God is universal love.
2 Jesus modelled this divine love and thus his (later) Christ-persona is a picture of a universal image of incarnated divine love, totally inclusive and generous to all.
3 Any form of belief, Christian, Pagan or other, that limits this, in any way, is not good for my soul.

* * *

It's beautiful down *The Grange* today. I'm near the standing stones on the way to the riverside walk. And I'm totally awestruck by the picture postcard look of it all, sun shining, blue sky, frost and sugar icing snow painting the whole landscape brilliant white.

I'm contemplating a recent telephone discussion I had with a particular high profile liberal Anglican priest. I told him about my green light from the bishop and he surprised me by his advice; surprised not so much by the fact that he encouraged me to accept the offer, but the way he expressed it. He said that it's now time for me to come back in and that I needed to get a "living" think about my pension and basically do the job and try to be as invisible as possible. I could see that he was talking out of concern for me and my family, but I was unsettled by his taking for granted that I'd need to silence myself were I to be a Church of England cleric again, and that this would be an appropriate way forward! After all I'd been through as a direct consequence of a stand for authenticity, how could I possibly start compromising and living an unreal life again? What would the cost be to my spiritual health, to my soul? Perhaps this conversation taught me more than any other advice I had received.

The synchronicity leaves me speechless! I've just arrived home from my run and the moon was full. She hung up there in blue dawn sky, and as I stood looking up at her I heard that all too familiar "croak" and, sure enough, my soul friend turned up out of the blue. A huge, silky blue-black angel, almost in slow motion, passed gracefully across the moon above me. She must have only been about thirty feet away from me. What a sight!

* * *

(The day after Boxing Day)

I woke up this morning, Boxing Day's headache almost gone, feeling the need to attend church. I had planned on going to Midnight Mass this year but I was just too tired in the end. However today I wondered whether to brave my old church The Priory, but decided against it considering All Saints Hereford to be a safer option (I love The Priory and have many friends here but I still get growled at by some).

However as I drove towards Hereford I found the wizard calling to me. The main Leominster to Hereford road takes me right past the forest where I wrote my book *The Wizard's Gift*. So I stopped and made my way to the Reading Chair.

I'm now here, cup of hot chocolate in my hand, standing under the double-headed god (Janus I think) engraved on the ceiling of the rune chiseled Reading Chair. On the way up the frozen slippery path I saw a silent buzzard sailing up there above and a pheasant scurrying around below, a bird of the air and a bird of the earth. Birds "speak" to me, the raven (my inner guide) has called me here today.

I performed a little ritual and sat waiting for the voice. Then it came:

Mark, little brother, do not fear.

Be still, be open, be brave and write these words, for they are your own wisdom made visible.

How many other people have you asked advice from lately?

And how many of them have soothed your whirling mind?

Not one. Why?

Certainly not because they are unwise.

No, every one of them spoke depth and meaning, but they cannot bring you peace because peace is only yours to unlock and own.

Mark you have the answers, so listen to your deepest Self.

Here you stand under the faces of a double headed god.

Look up and notice that he looks in two directions, yet one direction is covered with green erosion, whereas the other is clear.

It is clear and bright and looking over to the West.

To the sign of Water which represents the heart and emotions.

His other face is looking to the East, the way of Air, and of the head and thoughts.

Mark you've spent far too long in the head now, trying to think your way out of everything.

Now begin to trust your heart, your feelings, and your gut (instincts) too.

These two directions are the conflict within you.

Give your mind a break and trust in the love that carries you.

Don't worry so much about the "what ifs." Live with the excitement of the "daily gifts."

You will always seek to feed your mind. Each week more and more books end up on your bedside table.

That's good. It's good to absorb knowledge but knowledge is not wisdom.

The deepest wisdom comes from a well much deeper than the rational mind.

Mark your lesson to yourself for today and for the New Year is this, let go of worry. All will be well.

Let go of your concerns about the church and whether or not to re-enter official ministry.

Remain part of it if you can honestly do so, but do not expect that you can go back to how it once was. This will just result in more un-peace and mental unrest. Remain free.

With the god above you look now in just one direction. Choose your path. Be either a Christian who has a Pagan heart, or a Pagan who still loves Jesus, but don't attempt to be both.

Remain linked to any groups or organisations that feed you and do not cause confusion or feelings of hypocrisy. You can proudly and honestly belong to OBOD.

You can proudly and honestly belong to the Progressive Christian Network, but can you proudly and honestly belong to the Church of England the way it is?

If the answer to that makes you feel limited and uncomfortable then ask yourself why those feelings are there. Listen to your feelings.

Do not attempt to gain the "blessing" of an organisation or its representative whom you know you are not at one with spiritually. It will just put you back inside a straitjacket.

Enjoy the quiet and gentle way of the Druids. Do not clutter yourself with older ideologies you've grown out of and dispensed with.

Yes work on your projects. Your new book, but do not confuse work with the spiritual life.

Use your spiritual life as a place to unplug the mind, to simply be. And don't fear. I am always with you, I am the wizard, the inner voice, the Christ within, and I am the blue raven calling through the trees.

I will not confuse you and I will continually send you my signs as you continue to walk the way of the wizard, the way of deep synchronicity, oneness to Self and to ALL.

* * *

It's the last day of December, and it's become clear to me (at the close of a long year of soul-searching) that labels have become a distorted way of approaching the Divine and understand the Self. I will gradually try to let go of the impulse to indulge in all such categorisation. It is enough to simply say "I am me."

* * *

The last evening of the year was wonderful. I helped a good friend out at his hotel by performing some magic for his guests on New Year's Eve. And an amazing synchronicity occurred. One of my magic effects involves getting an audience member to secretly draw a picture without anyone (including me) knowing what they drew. I then have to try to determine what the picture is. However even before this part of the act I've already had a few other audience members come up with a random 3-5 digit number, by selecting a few number cards from a shuffled up deck. This number is then written out in large digits on a white board and left in full view. On this particular evening we were at the point in the performance when a woman had drawn a picture and I'd deduced that is was "emotional." I also went on to say that the image was of something or someone that is no longer alive. The woman gulped at this point. Then I asked her to close her eyes and focus on the image while I drew something on the white board, standing in front of it so no one could see it. I asked her to open her eyes and describe her picture. "A shaggy haired dog," she said. And I stepped away from the white board revealing a shaggy haired dog (drawn just under the four digit number from before). She and everyone else were adequately amazed. However, the icing on the cake came when I asked her what the dog's name was. She said, "He was called Jack and he was my most beloved pet. He died about ten years ago and I never stop thinking about him. He was like a child to me. I've never stopped feeling connected to him, and his name comes up all the time." I then asked her to get out a mobile phone if she had one on her. She did. "Ok I want you to imagine yourself sending a text message to someone about Jack. Can you do that?" She nodded. I continued, "Ok what four numbers on your mobile phone would you need to press to spell Jack?" She looked at her phone and then lifted her head saying "5225" as I stepped further away from the white board allowing the full shock to hit her and the audience. The four digit number written out above the picture of Jack the shaggy dog was 5225.

But the final piece of magic, the genuine synchronicity which shocked *me* more than any of the others, was yet to come. The woman said, through tears, "I never realised. I honestly never realised. I've been using Jack's name for years, probably from the time he died. My cash card's pin number is 5225."

You could have heard a pin drop!

Conclusion

Three more years in the life of a priest at the edge

It was a long haul, completing this book! I began three years prior to the writing of this *Conclusion*. Much more has happened since I first put pen to paper on that depressing January morning when the rug had been pulled from under my feet and I felt like a marionette figure in the hands of a mad puppeteer. I therefore offer this on the hope that it might answer any lingering questions with regard to what happened next. For example, did I go for the "orthodoxy test" and finally return to the ministry of the Church of England? Have I found a way of reconciling and harmonising my passion for Jesus with my Druidry? Did I ever get to publish the book I talked about *Jesus through Pagan Eyes*, and if so what was the reaction like?

To these and other questions we now turn.

Heretic! Yes or No?

So did I go for it? Yes I did. A short while after completing the December chapter of my year-long diary I decided to take the plunge and sit down with a ministerial training course Principal and theologian (from the Evangelical Anglican tradition) to be officially questioned about my beliefs. He'd been appointed to check me out in terms of whether I could honestly still claim to stand under the wide rim of what might be called the umbrella of Anglican orthodoxy. I looked forward to the experience immensely and saw it at least as much my own test to determine whether the Church of England was still broad enough to encompass me, as it was the Church of England testing whether I was theologically "safe" enough for them. I always relish the opportunity for such intense discussions because they tend to focus the mind and awaken natural discernment. Thus they can be quite revelatory. No matter how much thinking through possible lines of questioning beforehand, when it comes to the actual session and "being put on the spot" nothing can really prepare you for what comes out of your mouth (unless you're acting), and what *does* come out can be illuminating. So in a sense it was also *my* test to see whether I was still a Christian or not. *I needed to know.*

Before I met the theologian I mentioned the forthcoming test to a few of my liberal clergy friends, some of whom wanted to advise me with what to say and how to avoid (or skirt round) certain theological hot potatoes. But I was adamant that there was only one way forward, which was to be completely open and honest throughout. What would have been the point of all the struggle of the previous few years if I were to simply "cross my fingers and say the right thing?" Why go through so much turmoil as a consequence of honesty if I could now simply bullshit my way back into official ministry?

The conversation was amicable and enjoyable. I heard myself expressing what I still think of as a "generous orthodoxy." I know the Church of England well enough to be able to proudly affirm its Liberal/Progressive wing, whilst also genuinely appreciating its Catholic and Evangelical streams. I've always said that, though a liberal, there's a little of each of the three main traditions within me. And, as I pointed out to the man quizzing me, there are many Anglican clergy (including some bishops) who hold to a far more liberal position on matters of creedal beliefs than me. Also it has been long possible for Anglicans to subscribe to a metaphorical understanding of even the most central doctrines of faith like, for example, the Incarnation itself. I talked about my theological college days when it often seemed that I was one of the few students (and staff) that did believe in the literal Incarnation of God in Christ. I may have questions about that now, and I might have a semi-mythic interpretation of it, but no more than other liberals within the Anglican Church.

After the discussion the theologian's recommendation to my bishop was that, while it can be said that I am still broadly Anglican, I ought to deal with two other issues before having my license back. The first would be to attend church more often (fair enough) but the second would be to make a decision on which I really consider to be my spiritual home, in terms of Christianity or Druidry. That irritated me. For over two years I'd had the privilege of being part of a beautiful, welcoming Druid community and not once had any member of that community even began to suggest that I ought to choose between them and the church. It was simply taken for granted that I was a Christian priest and one who loved the Nature-based ways, and was therefore welcomed with open arms. No one tried to convert me, and yet here I was being asked to choose one way or the other *by the church*. I wrote to the bishop about that and he was very understanding.

In the end I was given what's called Permission to Officiate

(PTO) which was the right to exercise a public ministry again as a Church of England minister, but I was not yet licensed to an actual parish. I was very grateful for the PTO, though still unsure whether I actually wanted it.

Then came a life changing decision *(yes, another one)*. I'd been having serious inner debates about the PTO and was beginning to feel a pressure that I'd not experienced for almost three years, a pressure to conform. I detected it with regard to three different scenarios: my work as a freelance minister, my connection to the Pagan world and a romantic relationship that had begun a little after the orthodoxy test.

As a freelance cleric I'd enjoyed the privilege of conducting the most beautiful, open and eclectic ceremonies without any constraints. I'd officiated at a Druid/Hindu wedding in Richmond Park, London, handfasted a couple in a Christian-Pagan forest ceremony and performed a marriage blessing for a lesbian couple one of whom was a Catholic but who'd been banned from receiving communion for twelve years due to her sexuality. In fact, at their wedding I celebrated a full Catholic Mass and gave communion to the couple and their families. It was a very moving and healing experience. On this issue my inner voice was quietly whispering, *"Mark, you're not going to be able to do this anymore if you hold onto that PTO. If you're an official Church of England priest again you won't be allowed to do same-sex weddings."* It was not a comfortable thought.

With regard to my relationship to the Druid and Pagan world I was adamant that nothing would stop me from being connected to them, even if I was now an official Anglican priest again. And though that was true I did begin to detect a change in how I expressed myself, even on my Facebook page. I was gradually becoming conscious of my terminology and not in a healthy way. I was finding myself avoiding certain words or phrases that could make trouble for me (by that I mean trouble with my authorities). Again the inner voice muttered, *"Mark, how is this going to affect your writing? What about the freedom of expression? Can you really sacrifice it for the sake of being acceptable?"*

This made me feel very uncomfortable indeed. It was also during this period that a Pagan writer wrote a wonderfully generous article for the Church Times, in which she spoke generously and passionately about interfaith sharing and mutual appreciation. Yet a week later came the reader responses, and I was horrified by their negativity. There was also a response by a bishop which pointed to the official Church of England Policy on interfaith relations. I looked up the whole Policy and saw that it basically categorised Neo-Paganism as little more than a Cult.

And romance wise, I'd met a woman and had fallen in love with her. On the night we met we simply sat down together and talked right through until daylight and, after we'd parted, I wrote in my journal, *"I've just had the most romantic night of my life. I don't know if I'll see her again. I don't even know much about her. And even if I never do see her again I know I'll never forget her. Thank you God for showing me there's still love in this world."* We did meet again and are still together now. Her name is Sally and she's a gift from God (in fact I originally called her a gift from Persephone because this particular Greek goddess's story is one of death and resurrection/darkness and light, and it was from such utter darkness that came this gift of light). However, though I'd met and found love again, I was starting to feel anxious and tense. I was looking over my shoulder and worrying that people might gossip and make it difficult for us now that I was an official cleric again. I was concerned about being spied on and reported if my car was seen at her house too late in the evenings and other such stuff. In the end that was the final straw. I was not prepared to be put back in a straitjacket. How could I have gone through so much only to end up having to "keep my nose clean" just to hold onto my Anglican orders? So, one Monday morning I sat at my desk and wrote a very generous letter to the bishop, thanking him again for the PTO but stating that I'd decided to not only give it back but also resign my Anglican Orders too! I enclosed the PTO within the envelope, and took it to the Post Office. It was done.

The odd thing is that I had begun to feel more like a Christian again, albeit one with a Druidic heart. So what was I to do? The answer was obvious – go Independent.

Deed of Relinquishment and the Open Episcopal Church

So, once I'd come to a decision to leave the Church of England, I found myself convinced that the way ahead was to join one of the many Independent churches. I'd been in contact with three main groups among the many "Indy" churches, The Liberal Catholic Apostolic Church, the Progressive Christian Alliance and the Open Episcopal Church. I thought a lot of each of them. In the end I decided to become a clergy member of the Progressive Christian Alliance (PCA). Progressive Christianity spoke my language and was flexible and eclectic enough to allow me to continue my spiritual adventure without any fear that I could stray too far. However I also knew deep down that I was still an Anglican at heart and that I also valued the principal and practise of the threefold ministry (Deacon, Priest/Presbyter, and Bishop). While my own place within such a threefold order had not been a very pleasant experience I figured that that was mainly due to personalities within the system rather that the system itself. I also felt that, if I were to relaunch a visible layer of accountability and pastoral oversight over me. The PCA does not have "Episcopal oversight" and most of its clergy are based in America. And, though I loved the PCA and had no intention of leaving them, I also knew that I needed a more local church community as well. Out of the two possible Episcopal Indy churches, The Liberal Catholic Church and the Open Episcopal Church, I decided to seek Incardination (a transferral of my priestly orders) within the latter, for it seemed to have a very Anglican feel and was clearly the most open in terms of allowing each cleric to find their own way within the spectrum of theological, ecclesiastical, liturgical and spiritual beliefs and practises.

The process took over a year because to free myself from the Church of England legally I had to apply for a "Deed of Relinquishment" which effectively severed my orders from the established church. I was then re-ordained within a beautiful ceremony in my home town of Leominster officiated by the Archbishop of the Open Episcopal Church, Archbishop Jonathan Blake. Jonathan and I had got to know each other over the previous few years and I had grown to respect and appreciate his warmth, generosity and open spirit immensely. The ordination service was attended by over 100 people from various Christian denominations as well as many Pagans. In fact both multi-denominational Christian and Pagan Clergy were involved in the service itself. The final blessing for my new ministry was given by a priestess of the Goddess and a Druid Chief which, I imagine, is the first time that's ever happened within the history of Christian ordinations.

So, I'd finally done it. I'd completed the circle. I'd discovered how to re-ignite my Christian priesthood as well as remain thoroughly plugged into the rich and earthy beauty of the Pagan world. I'd found the way - *my way.*

Discovering the Dude

Another highly positive aspect of my more recent spiritual travels has been the discovery of a movie; initially a "failed" movie which went on to become a cult film. I'm referring to *The Big Lebowski* from those trend setting movie-makers *The Coen Brothers.* Starring one of my very favourite actors, Jeff Bridges, the film tells the story of an all time Los Angeles "bum" called Jeffrey Lebowski but nicknamed the "Dude." One day the Dude's home is broken into and his rug is peed on by two mobsters who mistake him for a different Jeffrey Lebowski, a millionaire whose wife owes their boss big money. After talking it over with his equally eccentric friends the Dude pays a visit to the real Lebowski to ask for a little retribution for his soiled rug. He is consequently sucked into a hilarious saga where he ends up recruited to be the liaison between the real Lebowski and the captors of his kidnapped wife. The thing that stands the most about the Dude is his gentle and totally laid back way of dealing with almost anything. His motto is "take it easy man."

As I mentioned above the film eventually became a cult classic and now Jeff Bridges is probably equated with his role as the Dude, more than any other character he's played.

One of the many millions who've been inspired by the Dude's way of "take it easy, man" is a guy named Oliver Benjamin, and the Dude gave him an idea. He'd been a spiritual searcher for years but never really clicked with any specific religion. Yet he found in the character of the Dude something of a role model for life, a life that showed a middle finger to the aggressive and dog eat dog worlds of both capitalism and nihilism, seeing a better path as one which simply says "fuck it, take it easy man."

Thus *Dudeism* was born, and there are now tens of thousands of ordained Dudeist priests who basically try to follow the principles of the "world's slowest growing religion." I was Ordained a Dudeist a few years ago and I had the privilege of meeting Oli (aka The Dudely Lama) when he visited my home town with Thomas Fazi, an Italian film producer and his crew. They're currently making a global documentary on the Dudeist phenomena and they interviewed me up on my Reading Chair at the forest where I sit, reflect and write.

I'm mentioning this now for two reasons: 1) because Dudeism's philosophy adds something essential to my own anxious and often stressed out life. It gives me an image of a thoroughly chilled out way, which I need to work on (or should I say un-work on). And 2) Oliver's interview at the Reading Chair brought to light some perspectives that are worth sharing now. So here are some of the notes I wrote in preparation for that interview:

Why did I come back into a Christian denomination? What stopped me from abandoning it altogether and becoming a full blown Pagan Druid?

Well, while I consider the Druids and Wiccans I know to be among my closest and dearest friends, I still adore the man Jesus and the picture of God he seemed to portray. I still love the notion of the great God of Love, the God who *is* Love. In Paganism it's actually quite difficult to talk in terms of that kind of God. I adore the Pagan gods and goddesses, though I think of them (like any god-images) as strands, fragments, stones within a great mosaic. They're real in the sense that God/dess is real and he/she/it does seem to communicate through all the variety, mess and muddle of the polytheistic (and monotheistic) diversity. But I've not suddenly started believing in a different god, just because of my Pagan travels.

To me the Great All, the Source, the Creator is who I offer my prayers to, and it's that great Spirit to whom I've always prayed, though I have indeed used different names and expressions over the years. He/she/it is the Deity behind every religion and every metaphor. Saying that, I do not wish to give the impression that these metaphors are in any way "unreal." I guess I see them as refracted realities (energies) from the One Source.

So why not be a Unitarian then? Why still call myself a Christian?

Because the Jesus story is about two things: the human Jesus and the timeless Christ. In other words the Jesus story connects me to the Christ. The story didn't end on the cross. The human story of Jesus may have ended there, but the Christ story began there. The Christ story is the church's continual reflection upon (and plugging into) of the Jesus story. And the concept of The Trinity came via the church living out the continuation of the Christ story (of course it moves into metaphor around here).

If I were a Unitarian I'd stop at the historical Jesus, but I also feel a connection to the Christ, *the Living Christ*. This remained dormant within me for a few years, only occasionally rearing its head (the Sheffield Cathedral experience, the Rochester Evangelists Convention etc.) but now He's here pretty much continually within my mind and heart. On top of this I have always held onto a notion of the Holy Spirit as God-as-active-presence in the world.

So I'm still a Christian because I believe in the crucial importance of the man we call Jesus *and* because of the continual unfolding of that story through the (Cosmic) Christ of whom we are all part.

Why did I join the Open Episcopal Church?

Because the Church of England would not/could not have given me the freedom to express myself authentically or offer myself authentically. I needed a church community that was genuinely broad minded and open, not just a church that paid lip service to inclusivity.

I also needed a church that stands within the apostolic tradition and has a sacramental approach to liturgy. As an OEC priest I do not need to feel like I've changed my essential tradition. I was ordained by an Episcopal (Anglican) bishop in Hereford Cathedral back in June 1996. And I was re-connected to that ordination when ordained as an Open Episcopal priest in June 2011. Through the OEC I thus continue to live the *same* priestly calling and vocation.

Of course it goes without saying that I have no time for the notion that the Episcopal/Catholic tradition is any "better" (or more truly "Christian") than the Protestant/Reformed tradition.

It's just the pattern that works for me.

As well as being interviewed by Oli, Thomas and the crew, I was also interviewed for the Dudeist online newspaper (the Dudespaper). I'll add that here too because it says a little more about my "Dudeist" appreciation of Jesus.

An Interview for the DUDESPAPER
The Priest-Dude & Magic Man
By Revd. Tim Churchill (Dudeist Priest)

You might catch a glimpse of him in the shadowy background of his local pub, encircled by a fascinated and enchanted group of onlookers.

"What's happening?" you ask.

"It's the Priest-Dude," calls out the disinterested bar manager from across the room as he continues to wipe a beer glass dry. He's seen it all before, many times. But the crowd hasn't and neither have you. You step a little closer to the mystery. *Priest? What the fuck does he mean, priest?* You push yourself through the crowd and see for yourself. *Oh my God!*

There, sat with his hand stretched out on the wooden table, is the cause of all the excitement. A figure dressed like a druid in shabby woollen shirt and *Jesus sandals*, eyes half closed and a look of deep concentration on his face. You glance at all the expressions around the table. Their eyes are all focussed on the same place and you follow their gaze. Then you stop breathing for a moment. In the mysterious man's stretched out hand lies a spoon, but this spoon is moving. Damn it the spoon is curling upward as his hand stays still.

"Holy Shit!"

You and the crowd continue to watch as he tips the spoon onto the table. One young woman reaches out. She seems to expect a shock as she delicately touches it with the tip of her finger. It's ok. She picks it up. It's passed round and eventually you handle it yourself. You try and bend it.

"How the fuck did he do that?"

For the next hour or so you are transfixed by the mysteries you witness right in front of your eyes. He makes objects move, plucks memories out of your mind, tells you what word you are thinking of and even brings tears to some spectators' eyes; tears, not of sadness, but the joy of re-discovering their enchanted child within.

His magic is not like the conjuring tricks you've seen before. This guy seems different. He claims he is not psychic. He says it's a mixture of psychology and illusion. He claims he's not reading your mind but reading your personality from the subtle clues you give off. You don't know what to think and leave that night in an aura of spellbound wonder. You have touched a place within yourself that has not been visited for many years. Part of you wants to know how he did it but the bigger part wants to say with the mystery. You've met Rev. Mark Townsend, Priest-Dude & Magic Man, and you feel better for it.

Interview:

1) Mark you're a priest and a magician. Do you see any parallels between magic and religion? Is religion a sort of functional illusion, as Great Dude in History Kurt Vonnegut suggested?

In a sense, yeah, Vonnegut was right. Religion (every religion) at its best can make possible a real sense of connection to the great mystery beyond our comprehension. Whether there be an actual *Dude in the Sky* or not the cosmos is buzzing with creativity and natural magic. Religion, by ritual, metaphor and sacrament can plug us in to that reality. But it's not for everyone. Science, particularly cosmology and quantum psychics, can do the same, just as stage illusion can. I ain't kidding. Modern stage magicians are usually incredible skeptics and rightly so. They know how easy it is to dupe people. They can see how some of the more unscrupulous ministers use persuasive techniques (and sometimes even manipulative trickery) to con folk out of cash. But stage magicians ought not to throw the divine baby out with the "holy" bath water. Stage magic can be a priestly function. It can shock, enchant and awaken people to wonder in a way that much of religion has forgotten how to do. Bring back the mystery and awe I say.

Of course religion was born out of magic. It all began thousands of years ago around the shamanic camp fires, where ritual elders would perform magic tricks in order to awaken their tribes to the power of the universe.

2) Do you agree that Jesus was a Great Dude in History? Or is Dudeism a bit out of its element on that one?

Oh yeah Jesus was indeed the Mr. El Duderino of the first century. I've just finished writing a new book, which was all about stripping away the Christian vestments of this Galilean street teacher, to see what kind of a dude he really was. And to help me in my research I not only used the latest historical critical sources from the churchian world (we call it Jesus Quest scholarship) but also sought out a few dozen super cool writers of a world that is often seen as the antithesis to churchianity, Paganism. I interviewed many of the leading lights within the Druid, Wiccan and Heathen communities, and the Jesus of their imagination was a dude like you've never seen him before. With their insights, together with what I learned from the Jesus Quest, I was able to see Jesus as a counter cultural shaman/mystic whose essential message was *"Hey, don't let anyone try and put you in a box man and, like, never feel you gotta apologise for being who you are. You're special. In fact you're a god/goddess. And don't put me on a pedestal either. We're all brothers and sisters you know. The Dude up there is actually the Dude down here, inside every one of you."*

3) You're one of the most open-minded priests out there. What impels you to remain in the Christian fold? How do you distance yourself from all the baggage and associations of the established churches?

Well thank you. I guess I still stay within the Christian fold because I still love the main man (the first century El Duderino) and still feel that there's hidden treasure lying underneath all the crap and bullshit of the institution. But I left my own particular church (The Church of England) about this time last year because I ended up feeling I could be a better friend on the outside than within. I could have easily gone the Pagan way because I've made such great friends among them and have been awakened to the beauty and power of nature. But I'm still a priest and see no reason why I can't hold these two worlds together. So I've joined an Independent Catholic church (the OEC); one which allows me to be exactly who I am. Cool hey!

4) What insights and lessons do the Jesus of the Gospels and the Dude of Lebowski have in common?

Well can't you imagine this scene? The real way it happened. A reading from the Gospel According to St. Jeffrey chapter 8:

The tight assed teachers of the law brought in a woman caught in adultery. They made her stand before the group and said to Jesus, "Teacher, this woman was caught in the act of adultery. In the Law Moses commanded us to stone such women. Now what do you say?" But Jesus yawned and sat down on the dirt and began to doodle on the ground. When they kept on questioning him, he laboriously looked up, adjusted his shades, and said to their leader, "Hey lighten up man and, like, as if you are all perfect. Come on, you gotta treat the ladies with some respect. Otherwise what goes around comes around." Again he stooped down and wrote on the ground.

"But she's a sinner," said the guy with the coin purse held between his buttocks.

Jesus raised his head once more, brushed his matted hair out of his eyes and said, "Well that's just, like, your opinion man, now

233

leave her alone unless any of you can honestly say you're better than her." After that they bothered her no more.

5) Who are some other Great Dudes you admire?

Rather than rabbit on about my favourite long gone Dudes (like the Buddha and Francis of Assisi) I'm gonna just mention two modern day UK dudes who are giants in my life:

Peter Owen Jones, the coolest and most relevant priest in the Church of England today, famed for his amazing around the world adventures as an *Extreme Pilgrim*. Peter is unafraid to put his money where his mouth is and search for the divine spark in the most unexpected places.

And Philip Carr-Gomm, the inspirational hippy chief of the world's largest Druid order (OBOD). A man well versed in both native indigenous Western traditions as well as the mysticism of the Far East, especially Jainism. A truly fabulous dude!

6) What kinds of stuff do you like to sermonise about?

Well in a way I feel that the biggest need in the fast-paced and success oriented modern Western world is to slow the hell down, and to stop being so damned obsessed with success and perfection. I love the Navajo Indian rugs that have a deliberate imperfection sewn into them. They symbolise the necessary truth that perfection is the ability to include imperfection.

I also love to help people find their own inner gold, magic, wisdom. I actually believe we all have a wizard living inside us, a wise old man/woman who can guide us if we only slow down and listen. We don't need books or so-called sacred systems to tell us what to believe. We can be own teachers.

And I love to talk about the founder of my own tradition as a man who was often muddled and messy and pretty beaten up by life, yet he always managed to say the profoundest things. This is an example of my sermonising on him. It's from my book *The Path of the Blue Raven* (an adventure into the beauty of Nature-based traditions and perhaps the most Dudeist of all my books):

The story of Jesus begins in shit and ends in shit. In fact there's shit all the way through! If there was a historical birth scene in that "Little Town of Bethlehem," would it really be like the good old fashioned nativity plays our kids star in, or the over-sanitised Christmas card images? Don't get me wrong, all these images add to the magical nature of Christmas, and I'm all for that, but we mustn't see them as real. No, the actual story is not so quaint. It is however deeply relevant, for it's about a poor and homeless human family ending up in nothing more than an animal shack. No comfortable room with a bed. Just some dirty straw and a bucket of water. No fresh clean sheets and a cot. Just some old rags and a food trough. Think about the image. Apart from the parents, whose eyes would have first glimpsed this little one? Not the shepherds, nor the Magi, but those of the ox, ass and probably a rat or two. This is fantastic. It's a marvellously messy and muddled up picture of a "god who meets us in the shit," divinity intertwined with the animal muck! How native! How Celtic! How wonderful!

And what about the wandering preacher's final hours? Well the story tells of a gruesome experience; one load of shit after another. He was betrayed, rejected, beaten, spat upon, humiliated and then killed in the ugliest way possible. And the period between birth and death was not much better. He was misunderstood, called names, run out of town, viewed with suspicion and cursed with a group of total misfits who kept getting it wrong. This is a god-image who lives in the gutter rather than at the top of the ladder.

On top of this he also seemed to be able to single out other people who lived the shitiest lives; the beaten up by life, the marginalised, the unclean, the so called prostitutes and sinners. He befriended them with compassion and showed them a way out of their self-deprecating mess. And here's the really important part of the story. He didn't say "join a religion." He didn't say "believe in this or that doctrine." He would not even allow people to bow down to him, as if to say "don't look at me either." He enabled them to find a way out because he changed their view of the divine and he changed their view of themselves. He helped them to feel good about who they were; valued, special, loved.

And finally 7) So what's your essential message in a nutshell?

Easy. Accept what you cannot change. Change what you can. But, above all else, be yourself and look for the magic.

Personal Health

At the time of writing this postscript I can say that, with regard to my general state of health, I've probably never been fitter. I run and stretch daily. Yet I've also been in constant pain and/or physical discomfort for at least two years. Two years ago Sally and I enjoyed a lovely holiday on one of the Canary Islands. It was a fabulous week except for the fact that, half way through, I developed a headache which stayed for the remainder of the holiday. Back at home it lasted for two more weeks before I thought it was time to see a doctor. The GP assured me that a three week headache was nothing unusual and so I lived with it for another month before returning to the surgery and being given the same advice, don't worry it's perfectly normal and is probably merely a tension headache. In the end it lasted for a whole year and was constant, a deep throbbing pain in the back of my head, night and day. Over the course of that year I'd become accustomed to assuming that it was a "tension headache" and thus began running, stretching and meditating on a more regular basis. And, though the headache did finally fade away, it was replaced with something even more debilitating, light headedness and a sense of vertigo which was enough to make driving any further than a few miles completely impossible.

It's a real blow. I'm still suffering from it. For a year now I've had to be very careful which bookings I take because I either have to travel by train or ask Sally to drive me which seriously limits my capacity to earn a living. The negative side of my character occasionally decides that this is simply unfair and that, after struggling for four years to build up enough work to make a half decent living, only to then develop a condition that means I can't agree to the jobs can feel utterly despairing.

On the other hand it's taught me to appreciate what I do have a whole lot more. It's also teaching me how to trust in the bigger picture and not get overly worked up about things I have little or no control over. But it's hard.

Jesus through Pagan Eyes

I've mentioned a few times that I'd been working on a new book called *Jesus through Pagan Eyes*. Well, three years after receiving the contract it was finally published and ended up creating quite a stir within parts of the Pagan world, whereas (at the time of writing) the Christian world has by and large not noticed it. If anything I imagined it being the other way round. I understand Pagan apprehension about books on Jesus, really I do, but I was hoping that any criticism would be given after reading the book (or at least its introduction) rather than merely glancing at the title and making an opinion. If they had bothered to read my actual words they would have no reason whatsoever to suspect me (or warn others about me) as an undercover evangelist with dubious hidden motives. I also thought (perhaps naively) that the presence of so many worldwide and well respected Pagan authors within the book might add to its credibility within the Pagan world. This being said it has indeed been very well received by the majority of Pagans who have actually opened the cover.

Britain's Got Talent

What were the most memorable experiences I've had since I finished the diary? Well, one of the most eccentric (and possibly foolish) things I got myself into a couple of years ago was appearing on Britain's Got Talent (BGT), Simon Cowl's TV talent show.

I wouldn't normally have put myself in such a situation. However it was late autumn and I received an email quite out of the blue from a researcher for BGT. Apparently they were contacting a few magicians because magic had become the most scorned form of entertainment by the BGT judges, and the researchers apparently thought it was about time a magician or two really impressed them. Well I smiled as I read it and whispered "no way." However as the next few days went by I began thinking to myself that it might be one way to raise the profile on what I do and, if they interviewed me, I might even be able to talk a little about my journey and my spiritual beliefs. To cut a very long story short, the next January I heard that I've been chosen as one of the 500 or so acts to perform in front of the judges. Apparently my audition (as one of the 100,000 plus hopefuls) had gone well and I was set to meet three scary judges at a theatre in Birmingham. Terrifying!

When it came to the morning of the audition before the judges, nothing could have prepared me for the mixture of sheer overwhelming anxiety and extreme tiredness that I was to experience. Sally and I had arrived the night before and it hadn't been especially easy to sleep. We had to get up much earlier than the hotel breakfast and met outside the theatre front doors in the cold and dark Birmingham dawn.

There were only 20 acts performing and many were there out on the streets waiting to get in. The doors finally opened around 7am and we were ushered in. The filming began at that point and didn't stop until I left the building about 12 hours' later. I know, from previous TV things, that it always takes much longer than you imagine but this was unbelievable. By the time I finally got to perform I was absolutely exhausted, hungry and thirsty. Saying that, we were all very well looked after by the umpteen staff and crew members, and (though nerve racking) I found the experience very exciting. I also got to meet some very nice people. Ant and Dec were simply lovely. And Stephen Mulhern (fellow magician of course) was a delight. "I've got a good feeling about you," he said.

But I fell apart.

After all the pep talks and psyching up behind the stage, once I walked out to meet the judges and, more frighteningly, the audience I just went numb. I don't think I've ever been faced with such a hostile audience atmosphere. They were so tough. I could feel it. Amanda Holden was the judge appointed to ask me to introduce myself and I attempted a joke which rather fell flat. I had a deck of playing cards in my one hand and a huge toy six-legged insect in my other. I introduced them as my "Ant and Deck" (groan) but then immediately went on to self-deprecate myself. The effect I then attempted is something I do at almost every gig. I've performed it literally hundreds of times and it's a very strong piece of magic. However it *can* go wrong. It's the closest effect I do to *real* magic, because it genuinely relies on pure randomness. It didn't go right on this one occasion, typical. But I took a risk and the magic chose not to flow. I was buzzed by Michael Mcintyre, and right at the very end of my routine, by Amanda Holden. David Hasselhoff, on the other hand, said he liked the effect but none of them thought I should go on to the next stage. It was quite a let-down I must admit, mainly because I know I perform that effect most weeks of the year and to a much higher standard. However, the more I reflected on that scenario the more I realised what was going on. But before I talk about what I learned I must confess that, from my low standard performance, there was no way that I *should* have gone through to the next stage. It was dreadful to be frank.

Anyway, what I learned was this. When performing effects that do rely on a certain amount of "luck" (what I prefer to call synchronicity) you need to awaken or evoke a magical atmosphere *before* attempting them. I've performed that effect in many different environments and the Britain's Got Talent stage is the *only* place it has ever truly fallen apart. However, of the other scenarios there is a group of presentations that stand out (i.e. where it works with far less effort from me) and that is at my spiritual retreats or places where there has been a large amount of magical expectancy generated. These are the situations where I can be pretty confident that the effect will not only work but work in a near miraculous way. It's happened time and time again and, in these situations, I can add to the audience's experience by my utterly genuine display of pure wonder at the way the magic occurred. Of course most of the time my magic is geared towards purely secular audiences, and I've only ever performed once within such a hostile environment as Britain's Got Talent. So the effect has only ever gone wrong once, and it only occurs "miraculously" every so often, but it *always works powerfully*. What I've began to believe is that this is indeed an effect that somehow absorbs or takes on board the sense of magical expectation within the atmosphere. I can't explain it any other way.

The reason it did not work at BGT was because the atmosphere was unfriendly, un-enchanted and, if anything, out to trip me up (rather than me to mystifying them). And the reason why it works best within already spiritually/magically expectant situation is because somehow this atmosphere of faith/belief /wonder etc. encourages the synchronicity.

Where now doth the Blue Raven lead?

I don't think I'll ever feel truly settled, spiritually speaking. It seems that my own questioning and somewhat iconoclastic nature will always demand that I stay on the journey towards truth, rather than ever thinking I've arrived, though I must say that my years of struggle have given me much more of an insight into what various teachers call "living in the present."

At the moment I am more than content to remain a priest

within the Open Episcopal Church as well as a member of the Order of Bards, Ovates and Druids.

And so it's on with the adventure. I'm now beginning two new books, one which will be a Prayer Book for those "at the edge" and the other is going to be a short guide for those who see themselves as both Christian and Druidic.

I also have a future dream. My deep goal and passion is to (someday) be able to create a genuinely open and inclusive church *with its own building*, where people who've been squeezed out of the mainstream can come for unique and eclectic services and rituals. This church would also offer ceremonies for all those who cannot use a regular church for such events: gay weddings, inter-faith baby naming ceremonies, spiritual but not religious funerals and so on. But this is a long way off, not least because I'd need a sponsor in order to be able to afford such a project. *We all need to keep dreaming our dreams!*

So finally thank YOU dear readers, for staying with me this far. I do appreciate all the encouragement that I receive from those who read my books. Keep the letters coming. I love hearing from people who've gained something positive from my books.

Brightest blessings and warmest wishes to you all. And until we meet again, *bon voyage!*

Mark Townsend

Moon Books invites you to begin or deepen your encounter with Paganism, in all its rich, creative, flourishing forms.